Herefordshire Christmas

Compiled by David Green

ALAN SUTTON

First published in the United Kingdom in 1993
Alan Sutton Publishing Limited · Phoenix Mill · Far Thrupp
Stroud · Gloucestershire

First published in the United States of America in 1993
Alan Sutton Publishing Inc · 83 Washington Street · Dover
NH 03820

British Library Cataloguing in Publication Data

A catalogue record for this book is available from
the British Library.

ISBN 0-7509-0124-1

Library of Congress Cataloging in Publication Data applied
for

Cover illustration: Winter Scene *by Francois Valentin Gazard.*
(Photograph by The Bridgeman Art Library, London)

Typeset in Garamond 12/13.
Typesetting and origination by
Alan Sutton Publishing Limited.
Printed in Great Britain by
Redwood Books, Trowbridge, Wiltshire

Contents

The Reverend Francis Kilvert. His diary is 'a charming evocation of parochial life in the middle years of Victoria's reign'

from

Kilvert's Diary

FRANCIS KILVERT

The Reverend Francis Kilvert's detailed diary, recording day-to-day events in the 1870s during the last nine years of his life, is acknowledged to rank among the finest works of its kind in the English language. Although for four of those nine years he lived in his native Wiltshire, it is the Welsh borderlands around Clyro in Radnorshire and Bredwardine in Herefordshire – the so-called Kilvert Country – with which most people associate him. He was presented to the living of Bredwardine in 1877, where two years later – and just a month after his marriage – he died of peritonitis. The first of the Christmas diary entries reproduced here was written while Kilvert was still a curate at Clyro; the others were penned at Bredwardine, and like the rest of this remarkably perceptive and personal document, they combine to offer a charming evocation of parochial life in the middle years of Victoria's reign.

Sunday, Christmas Day, 1870

As I lay awake praying in the early morning, I thought I heard a sound of distant bells. It was an intense frost. I sat down in my bath upon a sheet of thick ice which broke in the middle into large pieces, whilst sharp points and jagged edges stuck all round the sides of the tub like chevaux de frise, not particularly comforting to the naked thighs and loins, for the keen ice cut like broken glass. The ice water stung and

scorched like fire. I had to collect the floating pieces of ice and pile them on a chair before I could use the sponge, and then I had to thaw the sponge in my hands for it was a mass of ice. The morning was most brilliant. Walked to the Sunday School with Gibbins, and the road sparkled with millions of rainbows, the seven colours gleaming in every glittering point of hoar frost. The church was very cold in spite of two roaring stove fires.

Monday, 23 December, 1878

Very hard frost. The Wye froze across below Bredwardine Bridge between the Vicarage garden and the Brobury Shore. It has been frozen over and the ice passable for some time at Moccas. Visited Priscilla Price and took her a pudding and some mince pies for Christmas. Snow deep on the hill.

Tuesday, Christmas Eve, 1878

Very hard frost. Brilliant sunshine on sparkling snow. After breakfast I went to the Old Weston to see the poor Davieses and comfort them concerning their child. On the road I met David Davies, the father, the shepherd at the Weston, on his way to the village to order the coffin, and to the churchyard to mark out the ground for the grave. He told me that it was not Andrew as I had been informed and supposed, but little Davie who was dead. The father seemed greatly distressed and indignant, because he thought the child's life had been thrown away by some mistake of the doctor. I went on to the house of mourning. Margaret Davies seemed very glad to see me, and her humble gratitude for my visit was most touching. She took me upstairs into the room where the dead child was lying on the bed, and turned down the sheet from his face.

I never saw death look so beautiful. There was no bandage round the chin. The pretty innocent child face looked as peaceful and natural as if the child were asleep, and the dark

curls lay upon the little pillow. I could hardly believe he was dead. Leaving the face still uncovered, the poor mother knelt with me by the little bedside while I prayed for them all. She was deeply touched and most humbly grateful. Before I left the room I stooped and kissed the child's forehead, and the mother did the same. It was as cold and as hard as marble. This is always a fresh surprise. I had not touched death for more than 30 years, and it brought back the sudden shock that I felt when, as a child, I was taken into a room at Hardenhuish Rectory where our little sister lay dead and was told to touch her hand.

Margaret Davies told me that before little Davie died he saw a number of people and some pretty children dancing in a beautiful garden and heard some sweet music. Then someone seems to have called him, for he answered, 'What do you want with me?' He also saw beautiful birds and the men of the Weston (who carried him to his funeral). He thought his little sister Margaret was throwing ice and snow on him (the snow fell on the coffin at the burial).

Wednesday, Christmas Day, 1878

Very hard frost last night. At Presteign the thermometer fell to 2 degrees, showing 30 degrees of frost. At Monnington it fell to 4. Last night is said to have been the coldest night for 100 years. The windows of the house and church were so thick with frost rime that we could not see out. We could not look through the church windows all day. Snow lay on the ground, and the day was dark and gloomy with a murky sky. A fair morning congregation considering the weather. By Miss Newton's special desire, Dora and I went to the cottage to eat our Christmas dinner at 1.30, immediately after the service.

Immediately after dinner I had to go back to the church, for the funeral of little Davie of the Old Weston who died on

Monday, was fixed for 2.15. The weather was dreadful, the snow driving in blinding clouds and the walking tiresome. Yet the funeral was only 20 minutes late. The Welcome Home, as it chimed softly and slowly to greet the little pilgrim coming to his rest, sounded bleared and muffled through the thick snowy air. The snow fell thickly all through the funeral service, and at the service by the grave a kind woman offered her umbrella which a kind young fellow came and held over my head. I asked the poor mourners to come in and rest and warm themselves, but they would not and went into church. The poor father, David Davies the shepherd, was crying bitterly for the loss of his little lamb. Owing to the funeral it was rather late before we began the afternoon service. There were very few people in church besides the mourners. The afternoon was very dark. I was obliged to move close to the great south window to read the lessons, and could hardly see, even then. I preached from Luke ii.7: 'There was no room for them in the inn', and connected the little bed in the churchyard in which we had laid Davie to rest, with the manger cradle at Bethlehem.

(The Dora referred to in this entry was Kilvert's sister).

New Year's Day, 1879

I sat up last night to watch the old year out and the new year in. The church bells rang at intervals all last night and all today. At 6 I went to Crafta Webb to begin my cottage lectures there. It was raining fast when I started, but when I got as far as the Common I noticed that the ground was white. At first I thought it was moonlight. Then I saw it was snow. At Crafta Webb the snowstorm was blinding and stifling, and I passed by Preece's cottage where I was going to hold the lecture, without seeing it in the thickness of the driving snow.

Before the lecture, I went in to see old John Williams. On

opening the door I was confronted by the motionless silent figure of a person veiled and wearing a conical cap, which I presently discovered to be a dead pig hanging up by its snout. John Williams deplored my being out in such a night, and said it was not fit for me. There were not many people at the service, but the usual faithful few.

When I came back the storm was worse and so thick and driving that I was glad I was between hedges and not out on the open hill. The young people at the servants' party seemed to be enjoying themselves with dancing and singing. After supper they came into the dining room to sing to me, each with a comical cap out of a cracker on her head.

The Weobley Goose

T.H. CHETWYND

T.H. Chetwynd's delightful anthology Poems of the Wye and Herefordshire District *was published in 1937 and contains a wide-ranging collection of poetic works reflecting the life of the region in its many moods. One memorable verse concerns the sad fate of the Weobley Goose – an emotive tale which could well dampen the enthusiasm of more than a few readers for their Christmas dinners!*

Oh goose, I pity thee poor thing!
A few short weeks to thee shall bring

A Herefordshire Christmas

Sad, sad mischance! Thy fatted form
To savoury dish shall they transform!

Alas, poor goose! Thou'rt prosperous now;
The gods with thee good things endow;
Well fed, well housed, thou knowest not
The horrors of their hellish plot!

Full gorged – but only for their greed,
Who on thy tasty flesh shall feed
Clean kept – 'tis but for their delight,
Whose craving keen thou shalt invite.

Thy inside they will stuff with sage;
Onions and breadcrumbs shall outrage
Thy lifeless carcase! Oh, poor goose
I feel for thee grief most profuse!

I seem to smell thy roasting flesh;
It doth my memory sweet refresh
Of Christmas last, when thy forbear
For us did furnish feast so rare.

Aroma rich the roast did yield;
A relish keen the taste revealed;
We licked our lips, and asked for more
From that fine dish's dwindling store.

Alas, grey goose! The weeks are short
In which thou still canst feed and sport:
Oh, well for thee thy dreadful doom
Lies deep within the future's womb!

But though thou'rt doomed to death, poor goose,
Till that sad time thou liv'st in truce;
Console thyself while still thou may'st,
Nor e'en one merry moment waste.

Yet thou shalt be avenged, grey goose;
Thy flesh so savoury shall induce
The pangs of indigestion dread –
Fit judgment for thy life that's fled.

The goose she answered never a word
To this my speech by pity stirred;
She stood and stared with wondering eyes
Into my face with pained surprise.

She thought some harmless lunatic
Was airing there his rhetoric;
'Twas plain my misplaced sympathy
Was wasted on vacuity.

'Tis ever thus! The wise man's warning
Becomes the butt of idle scorning.
We go our wilful way content;
Monition is but time misspent.

A Funny Old Quist

EVAN ROGERS

In 1978, as part of his series of biographies aptly entitled
Ordinary Lives, Clive Murphy recorded several perceptive
interviews with Evan Rogers, an octogenarian Herefordshire
gamekeeper who worked for sixty-eight years of his long life on one
estate – Brinsop Court. The result was A Funny Old Quist,
published three years later, in which Evan Rogers paints an
uninhibited and vivid picture of his childhood, his experiences of
the First World War, and his varied life as a gamekeeper which
gave him so much pleasure. During the Christmas period, a major
preoccupation for any gamekeeper has always been pitting his wits
against poachers, and Evan Rogers was certainly no exception –
neither was his father who had also been a gamekeeper on a
Herefordshire estate. In this first extract from his reminiscences,
Evan graphically recalls some of the more hazardous seasonal
exploits which his father had related to him.

At Wormsley, Squire Knight had a big rabbit warren, where
they bred hundreds of rabbits, an enclosure of about eighty
acres of derelict land – rocks and trees, too uneven for
cultivation – with a wire fence all the way round; once they
killed over a thousand rabbits to ten guns in one day.

Well, the poachers went there one night, just before a big
rabbit shoot, and run nets in the warren. Twelve o'clock, right

up on the boundary, Father heard a rattle at one of the gates. He went to investigate, and he woke up in a ditch next morning with his jaw out of joint and broken ribs. A cowman found him. What had happened was one of the poachers gave Father's big St Bernard puppy a clout and it limped home to The Pool House, and my mother thought, 'Oh, my husband is in trouble up the rabbit warren!' and ran about a mile and a half and contacted the bailiff. It amounted to my father going into Hereford General for seven months. The doctors gave him up and they sent him back home. Mother was giving him brandy, and any liquids she could make up, with a teaspoon.

All of a sudden, one day, his jaw come natural and he said, 'Mother,' he said, 'give me a lump of bread and cheese!' and he ate the lump of bread and cheese, and he recovered. Dr Hart-Smith of Leominster was amazed that Mother cured Father and saved his life.

The Christmas after – I've heard my father talk about it many a time – Tweed, the old keeper on the Foxley estate adjoining Wormsley, came to my father and said, 'Do come up and give me a hand,' he said. 'I'll be bound to have the poachers.'

Every Christmas Eve the poachers used to go on his estate and defy him to come out of his cottage. So Father went up after it got dark, to the cottage just under Nash Wood – I know every inch of it there – and they had a glass of whisky.

Bang, bang, bang! 'They've come!' Tweed said, and opened the latch of the door. Someone shouted out in his garden, 'Don't come out! We'll shoot you!' So he banged the door shut, and as he banged it, two charges from a twelve-bore come against the door, and the lead is in that woodwork today; you could cut the bits of lead out with a knife, though it's been painted a dozen times since then, and that's over eighty years ago; you can see the little rises of the lead where the paint goes over them.

That was the poachers in those days. They'd have their haul of birds and away they'd go in their ponies-and-traps. Now they come with a pick-up or a lorry where you're rearing game. And they still defy you to go out of your house! They watch you, and God help you if you go out. They'd kill you. We had a keeper round here shot dead the year before last. They couldn't care two hoots. They come with shot guns, revolvers, truncheons, any weapon they can get hold of.

This Christmas they've been coming for game in gangs of ten and twelve – and it's the same with these big turkey-factory places – *they've* had raids on their turkey houses and all. They take turkeys by the score; couldn't care less! Here, only three months ago – on a farm not far away – two bullocks were killed, eleven hundredweight each, their heads and their skins and their bowels left on the field, and their carcases gone – live animals at midnight! And sheep! Twenty at a time they'll take. What can you do? It's getting unbearable. That's what's happening now, these days, this present moment!

In this second extract from A Funny Old Quist, *Evan Rogers recalls how more than one festive dinner was assured during the first Christmas season following the end of the First World War. After his war service, he returned to the Brinsop Court estate, where he was appointed under-keeper to assist the head keeper, Harry Darling.*

Harry and myself, we celebrated the winter of 1918 in an unusual way. It was nearly mid-day, a fortnight from Christmas, and we'd been ferreting in Badnage Wood. We'd got our quota of rabbits; in fact, I'd paunched them and put them on a rail to carry home. Paunching made them lighter – it was a long way to go and we'd also got the ferret bags and a gun each.

'Oh, let's have our lunch!' said Harry. Well, we'd just finished our lunch and had a cup of coffee, when he said,

'Listen, Evin!' and I listened and I could hear an old sow down over the bank. She was going 'nrghh, nrghh, nrghh', and you could hear her little pigs answering her. She'd pigged out in the wood and her little pigs was about ten weeks old. She'd left Farmer Godsell's farm and he'd never missed her. Anyway, this great blue and white sow with big long ears and all her little pigs, whether she smelt us or what, she come up the bank and into the ride and, of course, we was amazed.

Harry Darling said to me, he said, 'Look Evin!' he said. 'Pork!' Up with his gun, Bang! He knocked one of these little pigs over, killed it outright. I've never seen an old sow run so fast in my life! She was going up and down with her legs running in the gallop, and her big ears flopping, and her little pigs, well, they was gone before you could say Jack Robinson.

My word, that little pig Harry shot weighed about thirty pound! 'I can manage the pig and my gun,' said Harry. 'I'm off as quick as I can,' he said. 'You can manage the rabbits, can't you? Take your time!' and he hurried past Round Oak, down across, and over a hedge half way along a meadow, and straight over the fence and into Ivy Cottage with this pig. I was following after, with the eighteen to twenty rabbits, the two bags of ferrets, the spade and my gun. When I got home, the lean-to shed was full of steam. Harry'd got the boiler going, bellied the pig, put it in and scalded it. Later we chained him to the beam of the shed where I now keeps my nets, left him to hang there till he was stiff, then cut him up and had pork all over the Christmas – I shall never forget it.

Harry Darling was down at The Bell over Christmas. In comes Farmer Godsell, and Harry tells him how he found his sow and piglets and sent them home to him. 'Do you know,' said the farmer, 'I've got that many pigs and piglets, I've lost count of them. There's a pound note!' – he gave the old keeper a pound for sending his pigs home. Harry didn't tell him he'd shot one of them!

A Christmas Tonic

SID WRIGHT

In the 1920s, Sid Wright was leading a busy life as managing director of the Herefordshire Fruit Company. He was also a regular columnist for various newspapers and magazines through which his thoughts about his family, his friends, his garden and his hobby of walking reached an increasingly wide readership. In 1941, many of his jottings were collected into an anthology and published under the title Shop Talks. *He wrote 'A Christmas Tonic' in 1923 for the Christmas issue of* The Grocer.

It's Christmas time, and to be in keeping I bethought myself that I ought to write something Christmassy. So I'm going to try and tell you about a December afternoon tramp which may inspire someone else to try such, as the very best of Christmas tonics, and one which will save any expense at the chemist's shop on Boxing Day.

It was half past one on a December afternoon, and with old comfortable clothes and boots I was on the road with my nose towards the country.

How strange the streets seemed. Everybody, I suppose, was having their Sunday dinner. Half-an-hour brought me to the Three Elms and a choice of routes, and I struck along the road towards Canon Pyon.

Twenty miles to the west, standing out bold, were the Black Mountains, and Hay Bluff was beautifully wreathed in

a rain cloud mantle. Up Bewdley Pitch and down the other side, and the wind that was blowing half a gale had brought the rain along with it, which made my face tingle as I journeyed along. Then it rained heavily, and I sat me down under the hedge, well protected by a great bunch of honesty. It soon cleared and the sun began to shine again as I turned to my left up a by-road rounding the hills that protect the fruit-growing districts of Burghill and Tillington.

Rounding Waterloo Farm and up an old track to the right, the path led straight up to the top, and then I turned me about and looking down the little valley in the fold of the hills – what a lovely picture was mine. The beautiful woodland scenery at my feet, Westhope Hill in the near distance, and away to the east the clear gleaming and glinting of Malvern Hills in the sunlight.

I must get along, however, and in a few minutes I caught up a boy and young lady and enquired the way to Tillington. Lucky for me that I found them – or they found me – because one had the choice of many paths at the top. We wound our way through the woods, and eventually emerged on to a woodside meadow, the boy leaving us to round up the sheep, and I was left with my fair companion.

Knowing this district very well 25 years ago, I enquired about all the people I remembered, and my young friend seemed rather curious as to who I could be, so I returned the compliment and asked her who she might be, and found that she was the dairy maid from the Court that we were now looking down on to – a wonderful moated Grange dating back into the Middle Ages, which is one of the wonders of the countryside.

So I thanked her for putting me safely on the right track, bade her 'Good Afternoon', and soon I was knocking at the door of Wood Cottage. The door was opened and a familiar voice exclaimed, 'Good gracious, we were just this minute

talking about you, and the jolly times we had', so I said, 'Talk of the angels and you are sure to see the glitter of their wings.' The fire was made up and the kettle boiled and we had tea together, and afterwards a homely chat round the fireside.

So much so, that I was very loath to leave, but I had to bestir myself and say 'Good Evening'. I was soon on the road, with the moon shining overhead, the hard frosty road under-feet, and a good six miles for home, which proved a most enjoyable walk.

There is no moral to this story that I know of, except it's recommended as a reliable Christmas tonic. So, without any more ado, I wish you all a very happy Christmas.

from

The Burton Court Recipes

HELEN J. SIMPSON

Burton Court at Eardisland near Leominster can justly be counted among the great historic houses of Herefordshire. The home of Lieutenant Commander Robert Simpson and his wife Helen, it is especially notable for its fourteenth-century Great

Hall and fascinating exhibition of period costumes, and attracts many thousands of visitors each year. In 1991, Helen Simpson compiled her book of Burton Court recipes, many of them based on food from her native Herefordshire. It provides, she says, 'a culinary journey through the whole period of Burton Court's existence, from the area's earliest settlers to the visit of Henry V, when Prince of Wales, in 1402, through to its Victorian heyday when no fewer than twenty-three servants were employed'. Reproduced here are just two of the recipes, both with the festive season very much in mind.

A KING'S CHRISTMAS PUDDING

This special recipe dates from the reign of King George I when it was used in the royal kitchens, and has been in the possession of the royal family ever since.

Burton Court at Eardisland

Ingredients (makes three puddings)

675 g or 1½ lb suet, (finely shredded)
450 g or 1 lb small raisins
450 g or 1 lb demerara sugar
450 g or 1 lb plums (stoned and cut in half)
110 g or 4 oz citron (cut into thin slices)
110 g or 4 oz candied peel (cut into thin slices)
1 teaspoon mixed spice
Half a grated nutmeg
2 teaspoons salt
450 g or 1 lb breadcrumbs
450 g or 1 lb sifted flour
450 g or 1 lb eggs (weighed in their shells)
A wineglass of brandy
Half a pint of milk

Method

(as printed in *The Daily Chronicle* in which the recipe appeared
in 1911)

'Beat the eggs to a froth, and then add to them half a pint of
new milk and mix the various ingredients. Let the mixture
stand for 12 hours in a cool place, and then put in moulds and
boil for eight hours. Three ordinary-sized puddings can be
made by any culinary member of a family from the
aforementioned recipe.'

BURTON COURT POPPY SEED PLAIT
AND CHRISTMAS STOLLEN BREAD

This recipe makes three poppy seed plaits and one small
Christmas stollen loaf, which is best served sliced and
buttered. In Germany, bakers begin to prepare their *stolle de
Noel*, the Christmas stollen bread, at the start of the festive

season. Traditionally, this recipe includes schnapps or brandy, almonds, orange and lemon peel, but this is a simplified version and I like to use almond paste.

Ingredients for the milk dough

1.35 kg or 3 lb strong plain flour
3 level teaspoons salt
55 g or 2 oz butter or margarine
30 g or 1 oz fresh yeast
300 ml or $^{1}/_{2}$ pint lukewarm water
600 ml or 1 pint lukewarm milk
2 standard eggs, beaten
2 tablespoons poppy or sesame seeds

For the stollen bread

Quarter of the dough as prepared below
15 g or $^{1}/_{2}$ oz melted butter
1 heaped teaspoon powdered cinnamon
Half teaspoon ground ginger
55 g or 2 oz whole hazelnuts
1 tablespoon soft brown sugar
25 g or 1 oz chopped flaked almonds
170 g or 6 oz ready-made white marzipan
Milk for glazing and a little extra melted butter.

Method

Sift the flour and salt into a bowl. Rub in the fat finely. Blend the yeast with a little water, then stir in the remaining water and milk. Make a well in the centre of the dry ingredients and pour in the yeast mixture and the beaten eggs.

Mix with the hand to form a soft dough, then using a kneading movement, beat well with the hand until the dough is elastic and smooth.

Helen Simpson, compiler of *The Burton Court Recipes*

First rising. Cover with greased cling-film or a damp towel and leave to rise in a warm place for about 45 minutes, until doubled in bulk. Risen dough will spring back when pressed lightly with a floured finger.

Second rising. Turn risen dough on to a lightly floured surface and knead well. Cut the dough into four equal pieces,

and then divide three of the quarters into three equal pieces. Roll the three equal pieces from each quarter into equal strips approximately the length of the baking sheet, and plait, so forming three plaited loaves. Leave to rise again on greased baking sheets, covered in airtight plastic bags or under a dome in a warm place until doubled in size. (The remaining dough is for the stollen bread.)

Heat oven to 450 °F, 230 °C, or gas mark 8. Place a steam pan of hot water in the oven.

Brush the loaves lightly with a little beaten egg, and sprinkle with poppy seeds or sesame seeds. Bake in the very hot oven for 20 to 25 minutes until well risen and golden brown, then cool on a wire rack.

Returning to the stollen bread, flatten the prepared dough into an oblong 14 inches by 8 inches.

Brush the melted butter over the surface to within one inch of the edges. Mix together the cinnamon, ginger and chopped flaked almonds, whole hazelnuts and the brown sugar, and sprinkle over the melted butter. Roll out the marzipan in icing sugar to about 12 inches by 6 inches, and place on top.

Roll up the dough so that it looks like a Swiss roll, starting with a short end and tuck the ends underneath. Put the roll into a greased 2 lb tin, or Pullman tin, and make four diagonal cuts a quarter of an inch deep on top of the roll, using a sharp knife.

Cover and leave under a dome shape for 20 minutes, or until well risen. Brush with milk to glaze.

Cook in a moderately hot oven, 400 °F, 200 °C, or gas mark 6, for 30 to 40 minutes until golden brown. Remove from the oven and brush all over with a little melted butter.

If you wish, you can brush it with a glaze made from 115 g or 4 oz sifted icing sugar, two tablespoons water, a squeeze of lemon juice and a quarter teaspoon of vanilla essence, and decorate it with cherries and chopped nuts.

Christmas at Fownhope

JILL JONES

*Herefordshire writer Jill Jones is on the teaching staff at
Hereford Cathedral School and is married to the Reverend
Prebendary Ray Howard-Jones, who was Vicar of Fownhope
and Brockhampton from 1970 to 1986. Her busy life at the
Vicarage during those sixteen years has produced a wealth of
memories, none more vivid than the Christmas reminiscences
related here.*

Sixteen Christmases at Fownhope Vicarage have now rolled
into one. They seem captured in a magic time warp.

During the Christmas period, the doorbell would ring
constantly. Frequently there was nobody there. Instead, a
present would be left on the step — sacks of potatoes, baskets
of apples, bottles of sherry, even a duck prepared for the oven.

I have to admit though, that when the churchwarden from
Brockhampton called one year with his seasonal offering — a
brace of pheasants — I wasn't too keen! He held them out to
me, their heads joined in death. There was nothing for it: I
must accept them graciously and touch them in the process.

Hooking my index finger under the bloodied string, I rushed
them to the larder, where they could hang out of sight. And
there they hung until, with both gloves firmly on, I hurried

them down to the butcher's shop which is conveniently next to the church. He gallantly undertook to prepare them for the oven, despite his own seasonal heavy work load.

A committed man, our butcher. You could see him working away at 2 o'clock in the morning if you happened to be out late. The unshaded light bulb in his freezing shop would also reveal his dedicated mother, Joyce, sitting at the counter writing the Christmas bills in fingerless woollen gloves. Although well past seventy, Joyce also still found the time and energy to clean the brasses in the church and arrange the flowers. Every Christmas she sent me a bunch of chrysanthemums to fit the colour scheme of my sitting room. When I changed my carpet, she evidently noted it during a Parochial Church Council meeting at the Vicarage, and that year chrysanthemums in the appropriate colour duly arrived.

It was Trill, Joyce's old school friend, who was usually the harbinger of our Christmases at Fownhope. Her beak and budgerigar shape accounted for her name, and she could be observed on Sundays at the parish communion, in her silk headscarf and fitted county tweed. A whiff of sherry confirmed identification. Sherry flowed in her veins, giving her a balmy fragrance appropriate to her season. Her voice was deep, cultured and slightly slurred. She had come down in the world, but remained proud of her county connections. She considered herself a cut above those who 'trade', but she was poorer than any shopkeeper I knew.

Two weeks before Christmas, Trill hired a taxi to bring her the two miles from her lonely rented cottage into the village to distribute her presents. There she'd be at the Vicarage door with gifts for all – our sons, ourselves and our parents, each one thoughtfully chosen, labelled and exquisitely wrapped. All this was done in bountiful style while the taxi's meter ticked away outside. We soon learned to have our gift to her ready and waiting at the bottom of the Christmas tree, which

we invariably hadn't finished decorating in time for her arrival. 'It's Trill,' we'd say on hearing her cultured drawl at the front door. 'It must be Christmas already!'

The Young Farmers were the next arrivals. They always let my husband, Ray, know when they were coming, so that we could stock up with cider, Coca-Cola and umpteen packets of crisps. Officially they were out carol singing. Bravely singing *The First Nowell* through to its shaky end was the traditional requirement before we let them in.

I can see them now, spilling inside the house, those who came last year cheerfully helping themselves to drinks, while those unfamiliar with the inside of the Vicarage, self-consciously study the furniture. Soon they are all at home, sprawling across the carpet and tucking into crisps with relish – and crumbs.

'Better sing another carol', is the leader's eventual reluctant instruction. Up they all get. We all join in a hearty rendering of *God Rest You Merry, Gentlemen*, a contrast to the quavering warble of a half-hour earlier at the front door. 'We wish you a Merry Christmas and a Happy New Year,' they sing, and off they go.

'What a mess!' I say to Ray who is already filling plastic sacks with their empties. 'They'll be in good voice for the carol service,' he replies.

The carol service is the Sunday before Christmas. The church smells of pine needles, the Christmas tree glows in the chancel, and beneath the pulpit, the crib scene seems empty without the Wise Men whose presence is forbidden until Epiphany.

From the vestry emerges the ginger-haired crucifer followed by the younger members of the choir in their red robes. Mandy and Wendy lead in, cherubic-faced inseparable cousins, whose ambition to be choristers dates almost from the cradle. Tall willowy Sarah walks beside sister Rachel, whose twinkling eyes and hat worn at a rakish angle are

Christmastime in Fownhope Church

deceptive. Hers is the outstanding voice that echoes resonantly against the ancient Norman stone.

The elderly choristers follow: tall, frail Joe Chamberlain, the dearly loved churchwarden, singing with all his might. No-one would know his ankle is still painful. Last Sunday, with typical concern, he waited at the lych-gate for Auntie Mary, our oldest inhabitant, to help her up the icy path. She wisely stayed at home. He slipped instead!

But a broken ankle won't keep him from the carol service or from reading the lesson. The doctor reads too, mumbling Micah into his boots and glad to get the ordeal over. No-one cares if they don't hear the words; the very presence of the village doctor is reassuring, for we are all his patients.

All too soon the mighty tide of an exhilarating *O Come All Ye Faithful* sweeps us out into the night. Christmas is almost here, bar a few more parish drinks parties – and more seasonal pleasantries exchanged, with one eye on the clock. There is so much to be done at home.

At last all the shopping is in and the family have all come home. Christmas is a family time after all, even in a vicarage.

It's Christmas Eve. 'We'll try to get back for Midnight Mass,' say my sons. They are driving now, and are off to Hereford, to the Green Dragon to meet their friends. 'If we don't make it, we'll take both the Grans to the family service tomorrow.'

I walk down the Vicarage drive alone in the cold moonlight. Ray has gone ahead to prepare for the service. The Grans are in bed. The church is floodlit; mumbling shadows bunch at the lych-gate; the village gathers for the service.

Inside the church there is that special hushed expectation peculiar to the Midnight Mass. Proud parents smile at me over the heads of offspring home for Christmas. The organ plays. The service is about to begin. I move up to make room for late-comers, when my sons slip into the pew beside me. Suddenly, and at last, Christmas is here.

Christmas Customs

A. LOWNDES MOIR

*Prebendary Arthur Lowndes Moir was a former vicar of the parish
of Bridstow near Ross-on-Wye. During his incumbency he
undertook a study of the origins of many of the traditions which
have come to be associated with our modern celebration of the
Christmas festival, and in his book* Christmas Customs *he puts
these into their historical perspective. In this extract from his
writings, he explains such familiar seasonal rituals as Christmas
greetings and decorations, and our annual preoccupation with
mistletoe, Christmas trees, yule-logs and ghost stories.*

'A HAPPY CHRISTMAS'

'A Happy Christmas' is the traditional greeting on Christmas
morning, and nobody seems to think of anything more original to
say. The happy Christmas has to follow the traditional lines, and
keep up its time-honoured customs. There must be presents and a
Christmas tree, decorations and holly, with an honoured place for
the mistletoe, and all the feasting of the Christmas dinner with its
turkey or roast beef. Stockings are hung up at the foot of the bed
on Christmas Eve, to be filled by the invisible Santa Claus, who
comes and goes by way of the chimney. Carols are sung by carol-
parties. The yule log should be blazing on the fire.

All these things go to create the right atmosphere for that
satisfying thing, an old-fashioned Christmas. They are quite

An early Christmas card, published in 1846 and believed to be
among the first ever issued

apart from the church celebrations, and are the ceremonies of
home. Here are customs which are kept unquestioningly just
because fathers and forefathers did so.

It comes as a surprise to learn that most of the Christmas
customs are of very ancient origin, and are a reproduction of
pagan Teutonic customs, mixed with some that have been
borrowed from the Roman feast of Saturn, called Saturnalia.

When Christianity was supplanting paganism in this
country, Pope Gregory wrote a letter to Augustine,
authorising him to retain pagan customs where possible and
give them a Christian significance. This accounts for the
survival of many practices dating back to long before the
birth of Christ and the Christian era.

The complete Christmas festival lasts from 25 December to 6
January, or in the language of the church, from the Nativity of our
Lord to the Epiphany, a period of twelve days, or ought we to

calculate it by nights so that the Christmas season ends on Twelfth Night?

Christmas morning dawns, cries of 'Happy Christmas' ring out. The old customs are to be repeated once again, and they may have greater interest if something is known of their meaning and origin.

DECORATIONS

Bring in the holly with reddest of berries, the twining ivy too, the laurel with its shining leaves, and anything else that is green.

There must be decorations for Christmas and they must be evergreen, the sign and symbol of perpetual life.

There was a time when Christian people hesitated to hang up evergreens as they celebrated Christmas, for this was a heathen practice. The pagan world used them when it kept high festival at the winter solstice, exulting in the ending of the reign of dark and desolate winter, and rejoicing in the prospect of spring, with renewed light and life.

The church quietened uneasy consciences, for with gracious tolerance and worldly wisdom, it incorporated this feature into the Christmas ceremonies, and the use of evergreens was sanctioned.

The commonest decoration is the holly. Following the injunction of Pope Gregory, a Christian interpretation was found for it. The prickly spike of the holly suggests a spear, and the red berries resemble drops of blood – like the blood that came from the side of Jesus that was pierced.

The ivy, graceful twining ivy, might be useful for the decorator, but a Christian significance was more difficult to find. For ivy was the emblem of Bacchus, the riotous God of Wine. It would be a pity to exclude ivy from Christmas decorations. A compromise was tried. Ivy was shut out of the house, and used only for exterior decoration, while privileged holly was allowed indoors. Quaint old carols reproduced the rivalry between the holly and the ivy, and at last a Christian

meaning was found to justify the admission of ivy into the home. As the clinging ivy needs support, so does frail man need divine support. But still ivy and Bacchus are linked! It seems incongruous at Christian festivities.

Laurel with its shining leaves can be included in the decorations with an easy conscience, for laurel stands for Victory and Triumph. A wreath of laurel leaves was the prize of the victors in the athletic contests of pagan times. To the Christian mind, the birth of Christ represents victory.

Rosemary has its place too. 'It is the herb sacred to remembrance, and therefore to friendship,' said Sir Thomas More. Its charm lies in its scent, for scent has a mystic power of recalling the memory of far-off things.

That other rose is welcome too, the Christmas rose, that bravely blossoms from December mud. This flower recalls the legend of a child of Bethlehem. A little girl followed the shepherds to the stable, longing to see the Baby, but she dared not enter for she had no present to give. Sorrowfully, she stood without, tears trickling down the little face forlorn, splashing to the ground. It was a sight to move Heaven's pity.

An angel came and asked the girl why she cried. 'I have no present, no present for the Baby,' confessed the girl, for she was very poor. 'Look down upon the ground,' said the angel, and lo, where those tears had fallen there sprang up plants, which blossomed as they grew. The girl understood; she picked a flower and took it in to the Baby, and the Baby smiled at His Christmas rose.

MISTLETOE

The most intriguing of the evergreen decorations is insignificant. It should be inconspicuous, and if invisible can be most effective. There is an art in placing the mistletoe where it can best fulfil its mission.

From the remotest times, the mistletoe caught the

imagination, with its green growth in winter on the apparently dead oak tree. It must be the soul of the tree, thought primitive man, proving that the dead-looking tree was alive.

The mystic Druids elaborated on the idea, and evolved a fitting ritual for the cutting of the mistletoe. On the sixth day of the moon, the Druids clad in white robes, cut it with a golden sickle, and it was caught before touching the ground in a fair linen cloth. Then it was carried home in a wagon drawn by two white bulls. The officiating priest wore a crown of oak leaves.

In this way the Druids perpetuated the cult of the mistletoe. The mistletoe bough probably had some connection with primitive marriage rites. It also brings to mind the old Norse myth about Balder.

Balder, rightly named the Beautiful, was the son of Odin, the war god. Frigg was his mother, goddess of fruitful earth. To protect her son from harm, Frigg took oaths from all living creatures, plants and metals, all that was on the earth or under the earth, that they would do no hurt to her son. All took the oath, save the mistletoe, slender and weak, that clung helplessly to the oak, and was neither on the earth nor under the earth.

There came a day when the gods assembled round Balder, and by way of compliment to his invulnerability, they flung stones and spears, and struck him with their swords, knowing their weapons were pledged not to harm him.

Only Hodur, the blind god, stood taking no part in the sport. 'Hodur,' whispered Loke, the evil spirit. 'You too should honour Balder by hurling a missile, to show it cannot hurt him.'

'But I am blind,' said Hodur, 'and besides, I have naught to throw.'

'Here is an arrow; let me direct your bow,' said the evil-minded Loke, fitting an arrow shaped from a mistletoe twig.

The arrow sped, with unerring aim, and pierced Balder. He fell to the ground, and with horror the gods saw that Balder the Beautiful was dead, slain by the fatal mistletoe.

His body was borne out to sea, in an empty burning ship, while all the world made lamentation – the gods and goddesses, animals, trees and plants. The pearl-like berries on the mistletoe were thought to be his mother's tears. Then because all the world lamented, Balder was restored to life again.

The purpose about the legend of Balder is clear. It signifies the winter death of the beauties of Nature, the period of dark grief. Then, as Balder revives, so spring is coming.

The story of the fatal mistletoe shaft, carelessly shot by a blind archer, gets mixed up with that of another archer, Cupid, who recklessly shoots his arrow while the victim stands beneath the mistletoe – expectantly!

The mistletoe is a symbol of life. Life is incomplete without love. Life and love – so the mistletoe fits in with Christmas after all.

THE CHRISTMAS TREE

The decorations of evergreens make an artistic setting for a spectacular feature of the Christmas festivities. There must be a Christmas tree, all brilliantly arrayed, adorned with candles, decked with ornaments and laden with gifts. The Christmas tree looks like a newcomer in the presence of the Druidical mistletoe and the ivy of Bacchus.

In a way it is, for it was only formally introduced into England in the nineteenth century. It may have appeared before that, but no-one deigned to notice it until it had had a royal reception in a royal home. The Christmas tree was set up by Prince Albert in Windsor Castle to the delight of Queen Victoria in 1841. From that time the Christmas tree became one of the most popular Christmas customs.

But how did Prince Albert get the idea? Obviously from Germany. The Christmas tree had been familiar there since the time of Luther. In fact, Luther, arch-enemy of ceremonial, is often credited with originating and authorising the

A decorated Christmas tree and the excitement of opening
Christmas stockings. This re-creation of a typical Victorian nursery
at Christmastime takes place each year in Hereford's Churchill
Museum as an educational project for local schoolchildren

worldwide ceremonial of the Christmas tree.

Where did Luther get the idea? What is the tree's real origin?

Is it derived from the palm tree of the Egypt of the
Pharoahs, the palm tree putting forth a new leaf each month,
with December showing the year complete? Or is there a
sanctity about trees which has made men regard them as
invisible manifestations of the divine?

Apart from pagan literature, the Bible tells of a tree of life, a tree of knowledge, of good and evil. God speaks to Moses from a burning bush, and Aaron's rod buds miraculously.

When Nativity plays were acted in the Middle Ages, it was usual for them to be preceded by Paradise plays. These showed Adam and Eve, and the tree of knowledge was brought in decked with ribbons and laden with apples.

If these origins be too abtruse, be content with the old German legend, told in various forms. The motherless children of a woodcutter lived in a hut in the forest. One day, while their father was away felling trees, the children heard a knock at the door. A visitor had come to the hut, a little boy, asking for food and shelter.

The children took him in and entertained him as best they could. They gave him the last piece of bread in the cupboard, and fitted up a rough bed for the night.

The next morning, on leaving, the boy-visitor planted a fir tree, and instantly it grew and grew, and miraculously brought forth apples and nuts and sweets in abundance.

Then the woodcutter's children knew that they had entertained the Christ-child unawares, and this was His gift.

Ever afterwards it became the custom to perpetuate the story by setting up a tree, at the Nativity, laden with wondrous things and named a Christmas tree.

THE YULE LOG

The word 'yule' is as puzzling as a Christmas riddle. What can be its origin? There are varied enterprising guesses and suggestions. Some say it comes from *iol*, the primitive word for 'wheel' – the revolving wheel, the turning year. The yule log is seasonable at 'the turn of the year'.

Or is it a relative of our word 'jolly', through the Anglo-Saxon *geol* or the Latin *jocus*?

Yet another venture is to connect it with 'to yodel', to sing

with pleasure at the sight of the blazing fire, in the spirit of the Biblical phrase, 'I have seen the fire, I am warm'.

The yule log had its own ceremonial. It had to be dragged home with fitting pomp and lit with a fragment of its predecessor which had been kept specially throughout the year.

The yule log was set ablaze at the midwinter festival; it was the symbol of victory over cold and darkness. Winter is conquered; spring and summer are even now on their way. The stir of the new year is about to begin again.

Yuletide is the darkest period of the year. Who would dare to venture out? Listen! The wind howls and screams, and then it moans – that mournful melancholy moaning of the winter wind. There must be, so thought the folk of olden times, messages in those voices from the darkness, perhaps of restless wandering spirits or the plaintive cries of lost souls.

Maybe Odin, fantastic spirit-god, was riding on the roaring

The age-old custom of gathering in the Christmas yule-log

storm, as Lord of the Yule, attended by the Valkyries hunting for souls of the dead.

This is the time of ghosts. Stir the yule log, let it blaze more brightly and shut out the unknown terrors of the black night.

Perhaps, after all, the spirits without are not unfriendly; they may be the spirits of the dead coming back to see the old home they loved so well. Let the house be cleaned and tidied, the cheerful log blazing on the hearth giving warmth and comfort. The spirits take a kindly interest in the old place; give them the welcome they deserve.

Even these days, ghost stories follow one another until a late hour round the Christmas hearth. The yuletide fire and ghosts seem to have had a connection from time immemorial.

from

The Diary of a Farmer's Wife

ANNE HUGHES

Anne Hughes lived on a remote Herefordshire farm in the late eighteenth century, and for a year – from 1796 to 1797 – she kept a diary of her daily life. A century later, this fascinating account was handed on by Anne's great-granddaughter to

A Herefordshire Christmas

*Jeanne Preston, a writer, through whose efforts it was
eventually published in serial form in* Farmer's Weekly *in
1796. In 1978, on Christmas Day, the BBC broadcast a film
based on Anne Hughes' life with her farmer husband John, as
recorded in her diary. The following extract, in which Anne's
original spelling and syntax are retained, relates to the
Christmas period in 1796, and is typical of the detail and
sincerity of this remarkable document.*

Dec. ye 15 – It have snowed so hard this 2 days, that we be
quite cut off from every body by the deep drifts. John and
shepherd did have to dig the sheep out which was burried
under the snow and make a road for them to walk home to the
yards. It do look verrie strange from the winders to see
nought but snow, it be verrie cold and the house verrie dark
with so much snow agen the walls. I be thankful there be
plentie to eat. I do pray there be no dum things cast away in
the snow. Carter and shepherd did have to dig their way to
work, and John's mother and Sarah did dig to the pigges and
calfs. The snow do make a bad mess on my clean kitchen
floors, but Sarah do clean with a will, so it not too bad. Bein
bussie I cannot write more now.

Dec. ye 19 – I have had no time for writing in my book for
sum days. The snow be all gone, and all the roads be deep in
mud, so that we out only on horse back and do put on our
patterns to sweep the yard place.

Carter's ladd be off for a soldier and a verrie good thing too,
for he will be safe and not trubble his mother any more. Tim
Prue be gone also, it were he who did make carter's ladd wild.

Farmer Jones did lose many sheep in the snow, and sum
pigges have been drowned in the flood water. I be glad ours
are all safe. John do say we on the hill, the water do run away
from us. It be but 6 days to Christmas, and I do hope the mud

will be all gone by then, for John's cusson Tom be cumming, and Emma and her ladd and his sweetheart. We have not heard how Mistress Prue and her sister have fared in the snow, but passon did come up on his grey cob to see how we do, and I verrilie believe it was mostly to see Sarah; but he did not, she being at the bed-making.

Later cums John all muddy and water dripping from his britches seat; he slipping up and sat in a great puddel when feeding the pigges. He verrie wroth and did romp about my clean kitchen floor which did vex me sore, but me knowing his temper did go warilie; so up to fetch his dry clothes, the while he out to the pump to wash the mud from his face and out of his hair. He better after a hot drink, out agen, me not daring to laff till he gone, albeit we fit to bust our selfes at John all muddy.

Yet I did laff too soon, for me and Sarah out to the pump for a pail of water, down I did go proper bump in the mud; me catching at Sarah, she down atop of me and the pail falling on her head; and thereat, John's mother out to see what all the cabbel be about, did laff much at me lying in the mud with Sarah atop, crowned with the pail.

Sarah laffing much, I do beg her to get off me to let me rise, so she up, still laffing, and me up, a sorrie spectacle too, with the muddy water dripping from my gown, and I did hurry in to get rid of it lest John should see and laff last after all.

We soon clean and tidy, and after we to the hemming of sheets, and John did mend some harness and divers things, then supper and to bed.

Dec. ye 23 – We have bin verrie bussie with sum goodlie things to eat. Boiled hams and great big mince pies and roast geese and hens and boiled and roasted beef, all reddie for eating. John's mother be going to make a pudden for carter and shepherd, and I shall give them a big mince pie and

Winter in rural Herefordshire: the River Lugg at Mordiford

apples, so that they can have Christmas fare. Carter's wiffe be cumming early to get ready for our visitors who be cumming tomorrow. We shall be verrie bussie, so I shall not have time to write in my book till all over.

John's mother have made a verrie pretty dish which she do call meat cake. She did mix flower and butter to a thick paste and put some on the bottom of a bake tin, this she did cover with the chopt beef and onion and herbs, then more paste, then more meat and flavouring, and paste agen, till the tin be full. Then she do cover all with more paste and cook till done. She do say this do cut like a cake when it be cold with the meat inside. There be also 2 roast hares and pudden with spices and plenty of apple pies and divers things and junkets, cider cake and cinnamon cakes and a rich Christmas cake, John's mother did bake.

I hope we shall have enough, but I be keeping sum rabbit pies and a big ham ready, in case it be wanted. John will tap

the new beer and the honey wine, and we shall have primy rose wine, as well as Eldernberrie, and dandie lyon, so there should be good store.

I do hear John below so must not write more; I do love my little book so do write much and have wrote nearly all the pages, and I dout if I shall start another one, though I do love it.

Dec. ye 27 – Christmas be all over now, and our visitors gone, but a right good time we did have, the roads did dry up a bit so not too bad for the travellers, who did cum pack horse. Cusson Tom and Emma, her ladd and his sweetheart Jan, did get here after a journie of hard going Christmas Eve, the rest did cum Christmas morning and all of us to church, leaving carter's wiffe and Sarah's sister Jane to help Sarah with the dinner to be all ready genst our cumming back, and mother and me did set the tables together in a row and cover them with my linnen table cloths; then we did put the silver and glass and all did look verrie fine. Passon did give a verrie good sermon, telling us to do to others as we would have them do to us, and the world a better place, to which I do agree. The singing did go right heartilie with a great roar, the church bein full, for all do like the young passon and his mother.

Then we out and home to our dinner. John did set at one end with the beef and geese, and Farmer Ellis at the other to cut up the hams and so on, which Sarah and Jane did carry round till all served, and all did eat their fill and had plentie. Then John did pass the wine and all did drink each other's healths; then the men did smoke while we ladies did drink our wine and talk of divers things that had happened through the year, not thinking so much had; then the men did say let us dance, so Bill and Jan did play a merrie jig on their fiddles and we did step it out finely; till all breathless, we do sit down laffing much.

Farmer Bliss did say let's have a story, so Passon did tell us a good one that did cause much merriment; then John did say he would tell them the story what happened when his father died . . . Then cusson Tom saying we be getting too serious, so Mistress Prue to the spinette to play a merrie tune, and we to dancing once more, stepping it right merrilie till Sarah do say it's time for tea; whereon we do sit down and do justice to all the good things provided, which did make a brave show and looked verrie good on the dishes; the lights from the tapers in John's mother's silver candle sticks did light the holly Sarah had put on the table in glasses. All the ladies did like mother's meat cake, and want to know how to make it.

Then we did gather together and play the game of Popp; we did put the chairs in a ringe, the men on one side, the ladies on the other with our hands behind, one holding an apple which be passed from one to another. The man must not speak but do beckon to the lady they think have got the apple; if she have not she do say 'popp' and the man do have to sit on the floor and pay forfitt, till all there; but if he be right he do take the ladie on his knees till the game be played out. After we did play bobbie apple, and snap draggon, the Passon burning his fingers mitilie to get Sarah's plum; all did enjoy it much, and then we did stop a while for sum cakes and wine, and sum songs sung by one and other; then more dancing till supper, then more games and later all home after a really good Christmas which we did all enjoy much with everybody happie.

from

Collected Poems

JOHN MASEFIELD

*Born in Ledbury in 1878, John Masefield is one of the most
celebrated poets of modern times, and for the last thirty-seven
years of his life – from 1930 to 1967 – he was Poet Laureate.
He was strongly influenced by the sea in much of his work –
both verse and prose – and there can be few who are not
familiar with his poem 'Sea Fever'. Far from his native
Ledbury, it is the sea which dominates the two Christmastide
poems reproduced here.*

CHRISTMAS EVE AT SEA

A wind is rustling 'south and soft',
Cooing a quiet country tune,
The calm sea sighs, and far aloft
The sails are ghostly in the moon.

Unquiet ripples lisp and purr,
A block there pipes and chirps i' the sheave,
The wheel-ropes jar, the reef-points stir
Faintly – and it is Christmas Eve.

The hushed sea seems to hold her breath,
And o'er the giddy, swaying spars,

A Christmas scene in John Masefield's native Ledbury: Church Lane
in the snow earlier this century

41

Silent and excellent as Death,
The dim blue skies are bright with stars.

Dear God – they shone in Palestine
Like this, and yon pale moon serene
Looked down among the lowing kine
On Mary and the Nazarene.

The angels called from deep to deep,
The burning heavens felt the thrill,
Startling the flocks of silly sheep
And lonely shepherds on the hill.

Tonight beneath the dripping bows
Where flashing bubbles burst and throng,
The bow-wash murmurs and sighs and soughs
A message from the angels' song.

The moon goes nodding down the west,
The drowsy helmsman strikes the bell;
Rex Judoeorum natus est,
I charge you, brothers, sing *Nowell, Nowell,*
Rex Judoeorum natus est.

CHRISTMAS, 1903

O, the sea breeze will be steady, and the tall ship's going
   trim,
And the dark blue skies are paling, and the white stars
   burning dim;
The long night watch is over, and the long sea-roving
   done,
And yonder light is the Start Point light, and yonder
   comes the sun.

O, we have been with the Spaniards, and far and long on
the sea;
But there are the twisted chimneys, and the gnarled old
inns on the quay.
The wind blows keen as the day breaks, the roofs are
white with the rime,
And the church bells ring as the sun comes up to call
men in to Prime.

The church bells rock and jangle, and there is peace on
the earth.
Peace and goodwill and plenty and Christmas games and
mirth.
O, the gold glints bright on the wind-vane as it shifts
above the squire's house,
And the water of the bar of Salcombe is muttering about
the bows.

O, the salt sea tide of Salcombe, it wrinkles into wisps of
foam,
And the church bells ring in Salcombe, to ring poor
sailors home.
The belfry rocks as the bells ring, the chimes are merry
as a song,
They ring home wandering sailors who have been
homeless long.

Christmastide in Old Herefordshire

JAMES DAVIES

*In 1877, the Reverend James Davies was one of the scholarly
speakers invited to address meetings of Herefordshire's celebrated
Woolhope Naturalist Field Club, a body concerned with the
natural history and archaeology of the county. Founded in
1851, the club is still in existence – better known today simply
as the Woolhope Club – and it meets regularly in Hereford.
The following seasonal extracts, penned in the pedantically
stilted style employed by so many Victorian writers, are from the
Reverend Davies's original paper, recorded in the regularly
published accounts of the club's transactions. He called his talk
'Old Herefordshire Customs'*

Although the overspread of railways has wrought such a
change in the speed of the march of intellect, that probably
not even the most old-fashioned English county can plead
ignorance of the meaning of the word 'obsolescence' – that is
the gradual dying-out of old customs – I consider that
Herefordshire, owing to its bad roads, absence of
manufactures on a large scale, and purely agricultural
population, must have had as good a field, both for possessing
and retaining such, as most.

If 'trade's unfeeling train', which in a non-natural sense

may for the nonce be taken to mean 'the iron horse', has now 'dispossessed the swain' of not a few of these, it is of less practical use to lament and regret them, than to endeavour to gather the remembrance of them into a pious record, and to discriminate between the good, bad and indifferent, to the end that those which are capable – as some certainly are – of being utilised and applied, may revive, at any rate in the memory, whilst the others may either, where harmless, though vulgar, give food for our educated complacency, or, where simply superstitious, minister, by their desuetude, to our practical growth of common sense and cultivation.

I do not doubt that many of the customs I am about to refer to, may have their counterparts in other counties, but it will not be supposed that Herefordshire's title to them is unreal or shadowy, if in each case I can cite a *locus in quo* within the limits or on the frontier and border of the county in which we are met.

To begin then with Christmas, and not to dwell on the 'waits', whose gatherings at this season, in other counties, are very graphically described in Mr Hardy's amusing novel *Under the Greenwood Tree*, and who seem to have given place, in many parts, to the carollers, who more considerately allow their well-to-do neighbours to sleep till six o'clock in the morning, there are one or two special Herefordshire customs about this season, which still, to our knowledge, survive.

On good St Thomas's Day (21 December), the old wives still go 'a-Thomasing', or, as Worcestershire folks would say, 'a-corning', in allusion to the custom both in that county and this, of their carrying a bag in which to receive in kind from the farmers and landowners, the contribution of corn, which is, we suspect, now generally commuted for a money dole.

It was in my recollection, in the neighbourhood of Kington, on this day that some of the old women who went 'a-Thomasing' used to bring the good lady of the court the

yarn which they had spun, and thereout to earn an honest penny in addition to the customary gratuity.

I doubt whether mumming is really at all indigenous to Herefordshire; and of course, the yule log, Christmas carol, and like Christmas customs are too universal to demand special notice.

Perhaps we ought to say, that Herefordshire yields to no county in the customary decking of its churches with ivy and holly at Christmastide. The mistletoe, though that is quite a special growth and almost a weed of the county, and not only furnishes truckloads to London, but finds its place in the kitchen, servants' hall and nursery of most of us, certainly does not help to deck our churches.

The Herefordshire historian Duncumb, affirms that on Christmas Day it was reckoned bad luck if a female was the first to enter the house in the morning, and the same custom, with variations, is found to have existed elsewhere. His explanation that 'all thrifty housewives should be at their own household affairs', seems scarcely a reason why the sterner sex should enjoy the monopoly of gadding about on this day especially.

Upon the feast of Stephen, it was, and still is on old-fashioned farms, a Herefordshire rule to bleed the cattle; as it was in the days of John Aubrey, the 17th-century chronicler, who, with his sire and kinsfolk, had property in Burghill and elsewhere in the county, to bleed also the cart horses. The true reason for this, is one which in these days we are sorry to find lost sight of.

A more curious custom was to be noticed in our boyhood, in several parts of this county, on the eve of Twelfth Day. I mean 'Burning the Bush'. At that time the custom was for all the servants of every farmer to assemble in one of the fields that had been sown with wheat. At the end of twelve lands they made twelve fires in a row, with straw, around one of which, larger than the rest, they drank a cheerful glass of cider

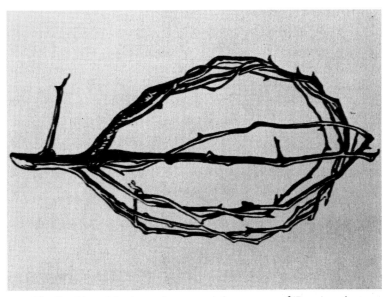

The 'bush' used in the ancient seasonal ceremony of 'Burning the Bush', was normally a branch of hawthorn bent into a roughly circular shape. This was believed by some to represent the orb of the reawakening sun, and by others to allude to Christ's crown of thorns

to their master's health, and then returned home to feast on cake made with carraways and soaked in cider.

Duncumb, who perhaps confuses this custom with 'wassailing', or 'health wishing' proper (because that is a feature in it) noted thirteen fires on the growing wheat, traces the custom to the Roman festival of Ceres, and adds the peculiar custom of the visit of the farmer and his household to the wainhouse on return from the field. Here a toast was proposed, a cake stuck on the horn of a favourite ox, which cake, according to whether the ox, when tickled, threw it fore or aft, became the property of the bailiff, or the lowest servant. The fires are said to represent the Saviour and His Twelve Apostles.

We have missed, in its order, an ancient custom which in some parts of Herefordshire (Duncumb specially mentions Dinedor) was associated with 'Holy Wells'. The subject of wells, and the honour and adoration paid to them by the heathen, for their supposed healing virtues, is large enough for a volume in itself. Here we are only at present concerned with what Duncumb says was a custom as regarded the well in Dinedor parish, in his day. 'Each New Year's Day there was a contest there for the first pailful of water, which was termed the "cream of the well", and presented to some neighbour as a mark of respect and pledge of good fortune.'

It is believed that the rivalry for the 'cream of the well' was an institution of long, long ago in Dinedor, but not in the memory of anyone now living.

In reciting our customs, a Herefordshire man would do wrong to make no mention of the Curfew Bell, as to the origin of which the general belief is that it was of Norman origin, in so far as it was William the Conqueror's enactment that all people should put out their fires and lights, and go to bed at the 8 o'clock bell.

Nothing is more common in the old record of parish charities than to find bequests of land or money to provide for the ringing of the 8 o'clock or 'couvre-feu' bell, and in the parish of Bromyard a curfew bell still rings every evening, for 15 minutes, at 8 pm, from 6 November to Christmas Day, the sixth bell then tolling the date of the month.

In many other parishes (for example, Leominster and Kington) a similar custom has been kept up within living memory, and akin to it, we make no doubt, is the custom of the bell ringing at 8 o'clock at night, for the guide and direction of travellers. I mention this because I believe the parish of Aymestrey has (or had) its night bell for the same purpose, and its legend of wanderers guided by it to the village's hospitable shelter.

A charity somewhat akin to this is that which appears to have existed at Thruxton in Herefordshire, where an acre of land, called the 'Bell Acre', was left towards the buying of bell-ropes annually, and there is a 'Bell-close' for the same purpose in the charity lands of Pembridge in this county also.

The Ghosts of Croft Castle

CHARLES CUNNINGHAM

Christmastide has long been the time for relating ghost stories. In the days when the yule-log blazed in an open fire, and the winter wind howled in the chimney and argued with the window panes, there was no better setting for the telling of a few spine-chilling tales of the supernatural. Even in these days when, for many of us, our Christmases are warmed by characterless radiators and night storage heaters, the custom still retains a certain popularity. Many of the great houses of Herefordshire are said to have their resident ghosts, and Croft Castle near Leominster is no exception. Traditionally, most ghost stories are based on occurrences which took place in centuries past, and they have often become blurred or embroidered with the passage of time. But among those associated with ancient Croft Castle are two extraordinary accounts relating to incidents within living memory, which writer Charles

Cunningham discovered when in 1992 he delved into some of Herefordshire's tales of mystery and imagination.

The history of Croft Castle and the Croft family can be traced back at least as far as the Domesday Book of 1086, although much of the present building dates from around the fourteenth and fifteenth centuries. The castle's long history is inextricably linked with many of the great events which have moulded the very destiny of the nation, and the building's strategic proximity to the Welsh border meant it was closely involved in the turbulent events of the fourteenth and fifteenth centuries when the Welsh and the English were at each other's throats.

With such a chequered past, it would be surprising if the Crofts and their historic home did not produce at least a few extraordinary stories of the unexpected, the unexplained, and – yes – even the supernatural. But oddly, it is from the present century, within living memory, that two of the strangest episodes belong.

Members of the Croft family still live in part of the castle, although it is now administered by the National Trust as one of the region's principal attractions for visitors. Occupying private apartments as a life tenant is Michael, second Lord Croft, and his sister, the Honourable Mrs Diana Uhlman. Their father, Brigadier General Sir Henry Page Croft, MP, who became first Lord Croft of Bournemouth, served under Sir Winston Churchill in the Second World War as Under-Secretary of State for War.

It was from Mrs Uhlman that I gleaned details of some decidedly strange goings-on which occurred in the 1920s, when the castle was occupied by her cousin, Sir James Croft, eleventh Baronet, and his mother.

Sir James was a keen sportsman, and at the time the events took place he was a rowing cox at Oxford. A house party had

been arranged at Croft Castle one winter's evening, and the assembled guests were due to go on to a hunt ball following dinner which they were enjoying in the castle's splendid dining room. Among the guests was a good friend of Sir James, one of his contemporaries at Oxford, a tall and athletic young man who was stroke for the Oxford rowing team. He had brought with him to the party a young lady who happened also to be a friend of Sir James's sister.

After the meal, they all adjourned to the Oak Room for coffee, where they chatted and smoked while they waited for their cars to be brought to the castle's main entrance ready for the journey to the hunt ball.

Eventually it was time to leave, and the guests made their way along the Gallery, through the main Hall and out to their waiting cars. It was at this point that the Oxford stroke suddenly realised that he had left his silver cigarette case in

Historic Croft Castle near Leominster, scene of strange phenomena within living memory

the Oak Room, and decided to go back to retrieve it. He hurried through the Hall and along the Gallery, and it was as he was approaching the door of the Oak Room that he collided heavily with a figure who was standing there in the shadows. About to make his profuse apologies for his clumsy action, he was startled to discover that there was now no sign of anyone there at all. He looked round, and there was not even a servant to be seen. The Gallery, and the Oak Room beyond, were silent and empty.

Shocked and still feeling the effects of the collision, he ran back to the waiting cars, where the other guests immediately noticed that this usually robust and rational man – the archetypal Oxford oarsman – was now shaking uncontrollably, visibly pale and almost incoherent in his attempts to explain what had happened.

Subsequent investigation established that none of the guests was left in the castle when the young man went back for his cigarette case, and the servants had not been near the Gallery or the Oak Room at the time. It was equally certain that this normally level-headed Oxford undergraduate did not invent the incident. He could not have possibly faked his physical condition when he ran back to join the other guests.

There was only one explanation: he had encountered a Croft Castle ghost whose presence was thought by many to be perfectly understandable. It was almost certainly the great Welsh warlord Owen Glendower, who would have known the castle well, not only as the building played no small part in his warring campaigns in the fourteenth century, but because one of his daughters married Sir John Croft and thus became a member of this historic family.

A century later, the Crofts actually adopted the Welsh wyvern crest as part of their family arms, and the wounded black creature was probably an allusion to the Glendower descent and the final fate of this great Welsh leader. His ghost

would thus feel quite at home within Croft's ancient walls.

What makes this story all the more remarkable is the fact that it was related to Mrs Uhlman fifty years later, by someone who had actually been present when the encounter occurred – the young lady friend of the unfortunate guest from Oxford. She was still able to recall vividly the events of that momentous evening back in the 1920s, and could apparently never forget the effects of the deep shock her companion had suffered after his mysterious experience.

This same lady was also able to give Mrs Uhlman a first-hand account of another strange episode which occurred at Croft. It took place a few years after the Owen Glendower incident, and was also concerned with a house party one winter at the castle.

The guests were assembled in the Saloon amusing themselves with a session at the planchette board. As the evening progressed, they were awaiting the next spirit message to reveal itself, when there came a tapping on each of the windows, one after the other in succession. This, in itself, may not have caused too much consternation had it not been for the fact that the south-facing windows of this particular ground-floor room are some considerable height above the ground, with cellar space below them. It was obvious to the guests that the tapping could only have been accomplished either by someone carrying a long pole, or by a person whose height was of giant proportions. Neither explanation seemed acceptable. On the other hand, could it have been Owen Glendower's ghost again, trying to attract attention?

But before the guests could concern themselves further with the phenomenon, the planchette board started writing its next cryptic message. The words 'Croft must not destroy Croft' were spelt out, and a hush immediately descended upon the proceedings. Whether any of the guests knew the significance of the words is not clear, but it was abundantly

plain to the Croft family themselves.

For some time, in order to cut down on maintenance and heating costs, the impecunious family had been contemplating the demolition of a wing on the castle's north front, which is thought to have dated from around the sixteenth century. It was evidently a contentious issue, and possibly because of the implicit warning revealed by the planchette board, plans for the demolition were shelved and were not actually put into effect until 1937.

Thus Croft did, in effect, destroy Croft, although the circumstances which were to follow, may or may not have resulted from the planchette board's exhortation. Those seeking to justify the message could perhaps point to the fact that the family's impecunious state was not substantially altered, despite the intended savings which the demolition should have ensured. It also transpired that the castle was to change roles to become a convent during the Second World War, before being acquired by the National Trust in 1957.

But at least there are still Crofts living here today, if only as tenants, and the fine old building with its wealth of historic memories – and with what one hopes is Owen Glendower's benevolent presence – is in caring hands.

A Carol for the Cathedral

C. ALICE ELGAR

Both Sir Edward Elgar and his wife, Catherine Alice, had many associations with Herefordshire. Shortly before the Christmas of 1907, while they were holidaying in Rome, Lady Elgar wrote this Christmas carol especially for 'Dr Sinclair and the choristers of Hereford Cathedral'. She called it A Christmas Greeting, *and it was duly performed at one of the carol services held that year.*

I

Bowered on sloping hillside rise
In sunny glow, the purpling vine;
Beneath the greyer English skies,
In fair array, the red-gold apples shine.
To those in snow,
To those in sun,
Love is but one;
Hearts beat and glow
By oak or palm
Friends, in storm or calm.

Catherine Alice Elgar, wife of the great composer. Her carol 'A
Christmas Greeting' was written specially for performance in
Hereford Cathedral

II

On and on old Tiber speeds,
Dark with the weight of ancient crime;
Far north, through green and quiet meads,
Flows on the Wye in mist and silvering rime.
To those in snow, etc.

III

The pifferari wander far,
They seek the shrines, and hymn the peace
Which herald angels, 'neath the star,
Foretold the shepherds, bidding strife to cease.
To those in snow, etc.

IV

Our England sleeps in shroud of snow,
Bells, sadly sweet, knell life's swift flight,
And tears, unbid, are wont to flow,
As 'Noel! Noel!' sounds across the night.
To those in snow, etc.

C. ALICE ELGAR
Rome, Dec. 1907

from

Daughter of Wyedean and Kernow

JESSIE M. STONHAM

Jessie Stonham was born at Ross-on-Wye and lived for most of her younger days at nearby Weston-under-Penyard. In the 1970s she wrote Daughter of Wyedean and Kernow, *a delightful account of her childhood in the early years of the century, in which she includes vivid recollections of her early life in Herefordshire. She also weaves in memories of times spent at her relatives' homes in the Forest of Dean and in Cornwall, a county she calls by its old Cornish name of Kernow in her book's title. In the following extract she remembers some of her family's festive traditions which helped to make her childhood Christmases in Herefordshire so special.*

Christmas can never be 'a thing of the past', but there are some things associated with it which have greatly changed. For instance, there were presents in our Christmas stockings which are seldom, if ever, seen these days. There were wooden jointed dolls with painted faces, and the 'monkey-up-a-stick',

also beautifully painted and giving much pleasure. There were also other clever toys made of wood, which were imported, I believe, from the continent. We always looked forward to finding among the smaller items in our stockings, a sugar mouse, sixpenny pieces, and several kinds of nuts in the toe.

Christmas was a wonderful time for us when we were small children. My mother saw to the decorating and, with my aunt, she did the purchasing and preparation of the special Christmas food. But it was my father who went to no end of trouble to arrange pleasant surprises of one kind or another, and to see that we had an enjoyable time. He did the stocking-filling, and on one Christmas morning, he informed us that Father Christmas must have had a hole in his sack. When we came to look in our stockings we found a trail of little toys, nuts and other small items, all the way from where they were hanging, right into the fireplace. This made us very sure that Father Christmas had been down our chimney, and the belief remained for a long time.

The Christmas pudding had an importance all its own. Like the mincemeat, it had been prepared in the autumn and much labour was involved. Fruit was not pre-packed as it is today, but was sold loose. Raisins, currants and sultanas had to be cleaned and 'stalked', and in the case of the raisins, their pips removed. They were then washed, dried and set aside. Halves of crystallized oranges and lemons were chopped into small pieces. All the fruit was then added to the dry ingredients. Children loved helping with these chores, and much fruit disappeared into tiny mouths before it could reach the pudding mixture!

At this stage, the silver sixpenny pieces and charms, previously washed, were put in, and after the wet ingredients had been added, everyone would 'have a stir' before the mixture was put into greased basins and covered with greaseproof paper.

Finally, the basins were tied down with pudding cloths, the four corners of which were tied on top.

The mincemeat was also made in a similar way, and was packed away in large earthenware jars until needed for the tarts and pastries.

When the time arrived, on Christmas Day, the pudding was brought to the table apparently in flames, and with a sprig of holly stuck in the top. Brandy or some other spirit had been poured over it and then set alight before the dish was held aloft and carried in with due ceremony.

If you were lucky – and the parent serving the pudding always saw that you were! – you would find a sixpence or a little silver charm, perhaps a horseshoe or a ring.

from

Lady Jenny

MARY HANNAH HERMAN

Set mainly in Herefordshire in the early years of the last century, Lady Jenny *is the delightful and often moving story of Jenny Gethin, a farmer's daughter, who is sent to work as under-housekeeper to the new local squire, young Francis Greville, at Mortimer Hall in the village of Bredsley. The servant-master relationship does not last long however. Jenny*

*falls in love with her shy, crippled and scholarly employer, and
when he asks her to marry him, she agrees, and embarks upon a
life which is very different from her innocent expectations. The
Christmas episode related here, takes place shortly after the
squire's proposal of marriage, although the betrothal was not to
be officially announced until after the festivities were over.*

On Christmas Eve the waits appeared, a little band of
countrymen and boys muffled in mittens and scarves and
floppy felt field-workers' hats. Their lanterns, borne aloft on
sticks, cast long wavering shadows over the frosty grass as the
candle flames shuddered in the wind. There was a mutter of
coughing and suppressed laughter, a scrape on the fiddle, and
then the singers and musicians set to with determination on
'The Holly and the Ivy'.

Jenny hurried to the bookroom to tell Francis they had
arrived and to urge him to invite them into the Hall for all
the household to enjoy their once-a-year performance. She felt
a little uncomfortable under his gaze. It was going to be
difficult to accommodate oneself to a husband who used so
few words when she had been brought up in a half-Welsh
family who rarely stopped talking to, across and against each
other. She fingered her apron nervously and found it pulled
from her hand. Then he swept off her cap.

'I'll need some moral support,' he said. 'You know these
people better than I do.'

'But Mr Greville, what will they say if I appear at your
side, without my cap?' And he hadn't given her any time to
tidy her hair, much less change her dress. Just like a man,
even if he were a gentleman.

Francis limped decisively out of the bookroom into the
great hall. The servants had come round the screen and stood
in a little knot near the end of the table, opposite the waits
who had made for the side nearer the fire. There were sidelong

glances and then careful blankness came over the faces as the Squire and his under-housekeeper trod towards them.

Mr Hewlett, the parish clerk, cleared his throat, the fiddle twanged, and they began again. Eyes rolled and there was the odd wink as the two young people moved closer together at the head of the table. They hadn't been going to sing 'God Bless the Master of this house, God Bless the Mistress too' out of deference to the poor young gentleman's solitary state. But old Will Turvey, who traded on his years as an excuse for his frequent lapse of behaviour, and who had, on their journey round the parish, drunk two pots of mulled ale to everyone else's one, wiped the dewdrop from his nose with the end of his scarf, and piped a quavering and audacious first line.

Jenny blushed and lowered her eyes as Francis quelled the incipient sly looks with his cold, grey stare. She hung back behind him, upset at this foretaste of difficulties to come.

This wouldn't do. She lifted her head and touched Francis's arm.

'I'll ask Simms to bring in the ale,' she whispered, and as she moved across to the servants, Francis motioned to Abbot, who handed a purse of coins to the parish clerk.

'Gor, that be 'eavy.' It was Will Turvey, forgetting his manners again, following the purse with his eyes, and snatching it from Mr Hewlett's hand to weigh it up and down in his own. Even he stopped short of opening it and counting before they got outside.

'Ha'n't been a hand-out like this — noo, not in livin' mem'ry, there ha'n't.' Mr Hewlett snatched the purse back quickly.

'Don't mind him, Sir. He's in his second childhood, with childish manners to match. We should like to thank you for your generosity, and we drink to your good health,' Mr Hewlett added as Simms appeared round the hall screen with a tray bearing a steaming bowl and tankards, and dishes of raisins and nuts.

'Ar, an' good 'unting.' Old Turvey reached for a tankard and raised it, his bright little eyes peering slyly over the top. 'An' yer can take that 'ow yer pleases, yer Honour,' he finished with a wheezy chuckle that ended in a bout of coughing, fortunately for him, so that, as his fellow singers thumped his back and remonstrated loudly and half-jokingly with him, the Squire's rebuke went unheard.

Then they all raised their tankards and the babble of cheerful banter ceased as Mr Hewlett gave the toast: 'The Squire, God bless him!' It was echoed by all those who saw personified in the new, young landowner, the leadership and economic stability that their little community had lacked for so long. Time he was taking a wife; Squire's wife could do a lot for the tenants and village folk if she was the right sort. It looked, though, as if he was hankering after sowing his wild oats with young Jenny Gethin. So went the thoughts behind the speculative glances as they drank up and replaced their tankards on the long table.

With much stamping of feet and touching of caps, they bade the Squire 'Merry Christmas' and shuffled cheerfully round the hall screen, throwing off greetings and witticisms to the servants.

They left behind an atmosphere of flatness and embarrassment; the relationship between Jenny and the other servants would never be quite the same. Should they still count her as one of themselves, or (if she really were the young Squire's mistress, as the more spiteful insinuated), treat her with an uneasy mixture of covert insolence and wary deference, as one who enjoyed the master's special favour?

On Christmas Day, Jenny had been going to meet her parents at the parish church, leaving Alice to prepare a cold collation to keep everyone going until Christmas dinner could be served in the late afternoon. But pleading that the feast for tenants and servants and their families, which she had persuaded Francis to

revive, would leave her with too much to do, she asked to stay behind while he headed the Hall party to the church.

'I'd like some time to myself,' she told him as she cleared the breakfast things around him. 'And I don't think I should be very comfortable with everyone's eye on me in a crowded church.'

Francis understood this feeling only too well. He closed the volume he had been reading and looked at her with amusement.

'I can see that the sooner we are married the better,' he said. 'I have no intention of letting the hoi polloi know my business before I choose; on the other hand, I don't want my future wife to be placed in an invidious position before a village-full of gossips. I suggest, therefore – er – my dear, we are married next month, as soon as the Christmas season is over. Abbott shall obtain a licence from Doctors' Commons so that we can be married without banns. So you can start getting your bride-clothes together as soon as may be. Call on Abbott for whatever funds you need.' He watched her changing expressions as she stood beside him with the tray.

'Oh, and by the way, I've a Christmas gift for you, a trifle; I hope it meets with your approval.'

Jenny put down the tray and as they were alone in the parlour, sank into a chair beside him.

'Sir – Mr Greville.' She still did not feel at ease enough to call him by his Christian name, and in spite of their betrothal, he did not invite intimacy. 'I'm fair – I'm quite overcome. I can't believe even now that we're really to be wed.'

She took one of his hands in hers. 'I'll be as frugal as I can, sir – my love. With the estate so run down, you've many calls upon your purse. Oh, what a confusion this is; I don't know whether I'm on my head or my heels.'

'Spend what you will, and see you get everything of the

best.' Francis ignored her outburst and rose from the table, still carrying his book, with his finger marking the place.

'Come,' he said, leading her out of the parlour into the bookroom. 'What do you think of this?' He picked up a painting leaning against the bookshelves, and set it up on the rent-table where the light could shine on it.

'It's a small thing by a local chap; Joseph Barber, I think his name is.'

Jenny looked at the little painting, a ruined castle on a hill, a wild, dark, autumn scene of wind and cloud, a moment of energy and movement frozen in time.

'Why, it's just like Leint Hill!' She caught her breath. That morning, their first time alone together, the morning she would remember all her life; he must have remembered it too.

'D'you think so?' he said airily. 'That's rather what I thought m'self.' Shyness clipped his speech. 'Thought you'd like something gothic; ruins and all that.'

She smiled tearfully at him. So he had remembered even their conversation.

'My dear, you couldn't have chosen anything that would give me more pleasure,' she whispered. 'Thank you and happy Christmas, happy Christmas.'

She took a deep breath, and leaning forward she took his hands in hers and kissed him gently.

Carols of the County

E.M. LEATHER AND R. VAUGHAN WILLIAMS

*At one time, long before the days of radio and television,
Christmas carols were often traditionally associated with
specific areas, and were rarely heard elsewhere. In the early
years of this century, Ella Mary Leather and Ralph Vaughan
Williams made a study of the words and tunes of carols being sung
in the neighbourhood of Weobley, and in order to preserve them and
afford them a wider appreciation, they were collected and
published, with music, in* Twelve Traditional Carols from
Herefordshire. *It is from this unique collection that the words of
the following two are taken. The first, entitled* The Holy Well,
came from gypsies in the village of Sutton St Nicholas.

THE HOLY WELL

As it fell out on a high holiday
On a holiday so high,
Sweet Jesus He asked of His own mother dear,
If He should go and play.

'To play, to play, dear Child,' she did say,
'It's time that You were gone,
And don't let me hear of complaint upon You
At night when You come home.'

'Now go You down to the merry little town
As far as the Holy Well,
And there You ask the children if they shall play
  with You,
And You shall play with them.'

'They say "We are lords' and ladies' sons,
And You the meanest of them all,
You are nothing but mild Mary's child
Born down in an ox-full stall.

"You are nothing but mild Mary's child,
Born down in an ox-full stall;
But You shall be crowned King of Heaven,
And the ruler above us all."'

The second carol from Twelve Traditional Carols from
Herefordshire *darkly hints at dire consequences for anyone who worked
on Christmas Day. Nowadays, with changing social and religious
attitudes and a more enlightened Church, such a brutal warning would
seem entirely out of place. The words of the carol were originally gleaned
from a Mrs Esther Smith, a villager from Dilwyn.*

ON CHRISTMAS DAY

On Christmas Day we forth did go
Down to the meadows for to plow.
As we were plowing all so fast,
Up came sweet Jesus Himself at last.

'O man, O man, why plow I pray
So hard upon the Lord's birthday?'
The farmer answered Him with speed,
'For the plow this day we have great need.'

His arms did quaver to and fro;
His arms did quaver, he could not plow;
The ground did open and took him in,
Before he could repent of sin.

His wife and children have no employ,
His beasts and cattle they pine and die,
His beasts and cattle they die away,
For the breaking of our Lord's birthday.

from

Tales of Old Ross

KATE E. RILEY

Many of the stories in Tales of Old Ross *— a book published
early this century and described by its author as 'fiction
founded on tradition and fact' — are devoted to episodes in the
remarkable life of John Kyrle, better known as 'the Man of
Ross', who died aged 87 in 1724. Immortalized through the
pen of the poet Alexander Pope, Kyrle served for a time as High
Sheriff of Herefordshire, but is primarily remembered — even to
this day — as the most generous, influential and respected
benefactor in Ross-on-Wye's long history. The following
Christmas story, which bears the title 'Geoffry Milbanke',*

*epitomizes the extraordinary compassion and unselfishness
which governed Kyrle's life, and it affords a fascinating glimpse
of the town of Ross in the early eighteenth century.*

It was Christmas Eve at Ross nearly two hundred years ago. There was snow upon the ground and a deep blue star-spangled sky overhead; the Market Place was thronged with people. Lights gleamed from the windows of the quaint old houses and threw rays of brightness across the snow. Every gable stood out distinctly – beautiful in its garb of white. There were booths in the streets, and vendors were noisily selling their wares.

Underneath the Market Hall – at the end nearest the river – there was a brisk auction going forward of fat poultry and other farm produce. At the other end a preacher was calling upon the people to think of better things than eating and drinking and enjoyment of life. Men and women, youths, maidens and children jostled and talked and laughed, and all seemed happy – except one.

Standing by one of the pillars of the Market Hall was a man of perhaps 30 years of age – a tall, thin, pale-faced man with cavernous eyes and large expressive mouth. He had listened to the preacher, he had watched the crowd, but he had spoken to no-one.

He was standing immediately opposite the house of the Man of Ross, and was being closely observed. At the window of his own sitting-room, John Kyrle was seated. He had been there for some time. The blinds had not been drawn, for John Kyrle loved to watch the life of the people in all its phases. In his hand was a volume of George Herbert, but he did not read much – his eyes were fixed almost constantly upon the moving crowds below.

The man who stood by the pillar of the Market Hall was unknown to John Kyrle, but something in the strange face

John Kyrle, the Man of Ross, from an early painting

arrested attention. The Man of Ross touched a little gong upon the table, and presently a woman servant entered the room.

'Come to the window, Anice,' he said, 'and tell me if thou knowest yonder man who is standing by the Market Hall – the man with the threadbare coat and miserable eyes.'

The woman looked. 'Aye, surely, Sir – 'tis the one who hath been about the town for several days. He came with his old mother who is a cripple, and took a small cottage in Dew's Court, down the Brookend.'

'Do you know his name?' asked the Man of Ross.

'Nay, Sir, he will not tell it; he is very poor; anyway, one can see that.'

'Yes, one can see that,' said John Kyrle sadly. 'You may go, Anice, thank you.'

The servant went away, and John Kyrle stepped across to a cabinet and unlocked it. Inside were little drawers, one of which he opened. There were several packets neatly labelled, lying there side by side, and these packets contained gold or silver or copper coins. John Kyrle touched them, one by one, and sighed. 'Nothing to spare,' he murmured, 'nothing to spare.'

He locked the cabinet and went to the window once more. The stranger was just turning away from the Market Hall. Instantly John Kyrle went downstairs, seized a cloak and hat that were hanging in the centre hall, and went out. He followed the man, walked briskly up to him and continued to keep alongside him.

'Good e'en, Sir!' said the Man of Ross, and at the same time he slightly raised his cap from his head.

The courtesy was returned, although the response was faintly uttered.

John Kyrle continued. 'Don't think I am unmannerly, in accosting a stranger thus. 'Tis Christmastide, and at such a time one likes to be friendly with all one's neighbours.'

'Do you count me a neighbour, Sir?' asked the man.

'Aye, to be sure, you live in Ross and so do I,' was the answer.

'I am but sojourning here for a while.'

'Nevertheless you are my neighbour for the time.'

'It is kind of you to say so.' The voice was spiritless.

'Have you known Ross before?' asked Master Kyrle.

The man's eyes flashed. 'I cannot answer questions, Sir,' he said, 'and with your permission I will say goodbye to you; my way is not yours.'

He turned abruptly into Dew's Court which they had by this time reached, and John Kyrle was left alone. He stood and pondered.

'A thoroughly unhappy, disappointed man,' he murmured, 'but not a bad man – no, not a bad man. A man of culture, too.'

He raised his eyes to the deep blue of the winter sky. 'God, why must it be?' he cried. 'Why must Thy people suffer? Why are we so powerless to help? What can I do? He refuses even a sympathetic word, and I have little else to offer. Money hath gone quickly of late – I dare not give more. There is but one way in which I could help him, but first I must know more about him.'

John Kyrle entered the court – glanced cautiously round to see that his new acquaintance was not in sight – and then made his way to a small house at the farther end. He knocked at the door, which was opened by a small maiden of six who, immediately she caught sight of the Man of Ross seized his stick and ran to hide it in a corner. John Kyrle laughed loudly.

'Why, little Meg,' he cried, 'art stealing my stick again? Dost wish to keep it?' The mother, a young buxom woman, came smiling forward. 'Nay, Master Kyrle,' she said, 'it is because she thinks to keep you here she hides the stick.'

John Kyrle sat down and drew the little one to his knee. His large hand rested lovingly on her golden hair. He shook

his head reprovingly, though his eyes smiled the while. 'Little Meg, little Meg,' he said, 'thou art beginning thy pranks betimes. Thou art a froward little maid. Why, dame, ten years from now we shall have to be thinking of her dowry!'

The woman's eyes grew tender. 'I shall not like to lose my only girl,' she said.

'Nathless, thou wilt have to lose her, dame,' said Master Kyrle, 'she will go the way her mother went before her, and repent as little, I hope.'

'Well, I've naught to complain of, Sir. My husband is a good man. He be gone to see the doings in the town and hath taken the boys with him. I and Maggie stayed at home to get ready the supper and hang up the holly and mistletoe.'

'Yes, look at our big mistletoe, Master Kyrle,' cried the child. 'Owen Jones did bring it last night.'

'And I must kiss you 'neath it before I go,' said the Man of Ross, 'but now I must to business. I have come to ask you something, dame, about a new neighbour of yours. Take a chair by the fire, and bring out those busy knitting needles of yours – that is if you can spare the time.'

'I can always spare time for you, Sir,' said the dame. 'I should be ungrateful if I could not.'

She seated herself as she had been bade. The bright firelight flickered about the room, touching the oaken dresser with its pewter plates, the golden hair of little Meg as she leaned against the Man of Ross, the knitting pins as they sped to and fro.

'I know who it is you would ask about, Master Kyrle,' said the dame. 'It is the poor gentleman who lives a few doors away.'

'Yes, I only heard of him tonight.'

'You have not seen him?'

'Yea,' said the Man of Ross, 'I saw him and spoke to him, but he seemed disinclined to talk. Well, what do you know of him?'

'Not much, of a surety,' said the dame, 'but such as it is I will tell you. About four days agone he brought his mother, an aged lady, to this poor little cottage and settled in quietly without help from anyone. They had a few sticks of furniture but nothing in the way of comforts. The mother never goes out, and the son only in the evenings. Last week I was walking down the court, and as I was passing the house, I saw their dog trying to get in at the door.'

'And can they afford to keep a dog?' asked John Kyrle.

'I'll tell you, Sir. I opened the door for the dog to go in, and the old lady called to me from her chair by the fire to thank me.'

'And you went in: ah, dame, I fear me you had been looking for an opportunity long enough,' said the Man of Ross, laughing.

'Well Master Kyrle, indeed I had, for look you, the poor things did seem so sadly that my heart ached for them.'

'Yes, yes, I know you would not have gone out of idle prying, Dame Williams. Now go on with your story.'

'Well Sir, the poor lady was so pleased to have someone to speak to, that she asked me to sit down, but of course I would not do that. I saw that she was far and away above me and I would not take advantage of her poverty.'

John Kyrle's eyes became misty and he looked at the dame half sadly.

'She may be above you as regards culture,' he said, 'but in naught else, in naught else.'

'She is a lady, Sir. She told me a little of her affairs. She has been a widow for many years, and her only son is an artist. He both paints and carves. From what she said I fancy he has had bad luck and not been able to sell much, and they have grown poorer from year to year.'

'Where do they come from?' asked John Kyrle.

'From Lancashire, I believe; the husband was a clergyman

there. But the lady, Madam Milbanke, is of Herefordshire birth. She told me that she was born in the Ewas Lacy Valley.'

'I wonder who she was,' mused the Man of Ross, 'but that does not matter – the question is how to help them. Do you think they lack food?'

'I fear me they do. No-one knoweth how they live. They are proud and cannot bear to show their poverty.'

'And the dog?' asked John Kyrle. 'How can they feed it?'

'It is my opinion, by going without some things themselves,' said the dame. 'The dog is old – it belonged to the father – they cannot part with it.'

John Kyrle rose. 'Something must be done, and quickly,' he said. 'I will go and try to gain admittance.'

'You have not kissed me 'neath the mistletoe,' cried little Maggie.

'Ah, now, that is a fine thing for a little maid to do – to remind me of my promise to kiss her. 'Deed I was right when I spoke of her dowry, Dame Williams,' said Master Kyrle. He lifted the child up in his strong arms underneath the huge mistletoe bough which hung from an oak beam in the centre of the ceiling, and kissed her rosy lips, then set her down gently by her mother.

'A sweet little maid,' he said. 'May she grow up as good as she is fair.' The mother smiled as she bade him adieu. She watched him down the street, a tall, strong upright man of fifty years or thereabouts. She watched him and sighed. 'One of God's own,' she said softly as she went back indoors. 'The best man I ever knew, and yet he hath none of the joys of life – none, except the joy of making others happy.'

The house at which John Kyrle stopped was a low-roofed timbered building, small and dreary looking. A faint light shone from the lower window, which was thinly curtained. He tapped at the door, and a weak voice bade him enter. He walked into a poor little room, scantily furnished. There was

A cold winter's evening at Ross-on-Wye, a scene dominated by the
historic parish church which John Kyrle's beneficence did so much
to preserve

but a handful of fire in the grate, and over it an old woman was crouching. She looked round as John Kyrle entered, expecting to see Dame Williams, and was surprised to find instead a tall elderly man in long coat and muffler, his boots covered with snow, his breath coming quickly from the contact with the frosty air. He took his hat from his head and approached her.

What was it in John Kyrle's expression that made the worn white face of the woman flush with emotion as she looked at him? What was it that made her weary eyes fill with sudden tears?

The Man of Ross did not speak for a moment – he simply stood and looked down upon her, but his look was one of such infinite compassion – compassion devoid of self-consciousness – that the poor woman's hitherto proud spirit was broken.

He spoke at last in a low soft voice, utterly unlike his usual loud, rather blustering tones. 'Forgive me for coming – I heard of your troubles – I want to help you.'

The woman turned her eyes towards a door which led to an inner room. She waved her hand towards it. 'Help *him* if you can,' she said. 'I shall need nothing long, but save *him*. He is a genius, but the world will not own it. He is dying of despair.'

'He will not die,' said the Man of Ross, softly. 'I will go to him.' He stepped across the room and knocked at the door. There was no answer. The door was a low one and at the top of it there was a space, for it was old and fitted badly. Through this space John Kyrle could see the wretched scene within. There was a narrow bed with scarcely any covering, a chair or two and a large old oaken table with a rush light on it in a wooden stand. There were several canvases with their faces towards the wall – palettes hanging on nails – and in a corner, on a shelf, some small pieces of carving in different stages of development – several tools lying about them.

At the table was seated the occupier of the room. He was

leaning forward – his arms stretched out – his head resting on them. By his side, upon the floor, was a dog – a thin hungry-looking animal whose nose rested upon his master's knee and whose large, loving eyes were fixed upon vacancy and filled with sorrow. There was a small packet on the table. John Kyrle looked at it and shuddered. Was the man alive?

Stout-hearted as was the Man of Ross, he trembled as he entered the room. Neither man nor dog stirred. He went up to them and placed his hand upon the man's shoulder. The dog uttered a low growl, then, looking up into John Kyrle's face and seeing there nothing but love and pity, he crept up to him and licked his hand. There was a slight movement in the bent figure, and Master Kyrle breathed more freely. The man was not dead.

'I have followed you here,' said John Kyrle, gently. 'I could not help it, for I saw you were in trouble. I am here to help you.'

The man roused himself and stood up, and the dog, with a whine of joy, leaped up at him and caressed him.

'That is a faithful animal,' said the Man of Ross, 'and one that hath understanding. He knows that I wish you well.'

'He knows everything,' was the answer. 'He is wiser than many human beings, and yet, when you came in, I was about to put him out of this life – I was going to poison him.'

John Kyrle did not ask any questions. He only looked at man and dog in silence. Then his whole manner changed. He spoke in his usual brisk, loud voice.

'You are not well,' he said. 'You look at things in a wrong way. You are miserable because you think you have failed in life. Man, this is nonsense. All work that is good for anything takes a long while to be acknowledged.'

'And whilst people wait, they starve,' said the young man.

'Sometimes, but, thank God, you will not do that.'

'Who is to prevent it?'

'I will.'

'Who are you?'

'I am a human being like yourself, but I happen to have a little money and I like to use it in my own way. I want you to stifle your pride, and for the sake of yonder old lady in the next room, take what I offer.'

'What do you offer?'

'First of all, creature comforts – your mother will die if she is left in this cold comfortless house much longer. There will be a sharper frost tonight than we have known for years. You must come to my house for the present – you, your mother and the dog.'

The man's face flushed. 'And accept charity,' he muttered.

'No,' said the Man of Ross, 'not charity but hospitality. You will be my guest, but even if it were charity, it would be no disgrace to you to take it. Listen!' He drew a chair towards him and sat down, then spoke more softly.

'Do you believe in the life of Christ who came into our world sixteen hundred years ago?'

'I know not: I used to believe,' was the answer.

'Have you lost faith in God's goodness?'

'I scarce can say. Life has been hard for me. Master, you know not what it is to go on toiling year after year, never gaining ground, meeting with disappointment, continually getting gleams of hope which are no sooner born than they die, struggling to be brave and to keep up heart even though you see your best beloved starving before your eyes. Master, how can you expect me to believe in God's goodness?'

'I will not ask you,' said John Kyrle. 'I will ask you if you believe in *human* love.'

'Why, yes, I *see* it working around me.'

'Then in the name of this human love which, after all, is a part of the Divine, accept what I offer.'

The man bowed his head and was silent, but John Kyrle knew that the victory was won.

'I will go home now,' he said, 'and in about an hour I will send a coach for your mother. You must come with her and bring the dog.'

'Why are you doing this?' asked the young man. 'We are strangers to you.'

'You would have done as much for me had our cases been reversed,' said John Kyrle.

'Mayhap I should, but I scarce think I could have taken such interest in strangers as you are doing. You must be a good man!'

'I – good? Nay, I am far from that. I am a rough man, harsh at times. I will tell thee a secret, young man. Long years ago I lost someone who was very dear to me – someone to whom I made a promise to "comfort the sad and distressed". I have tried to keep my promise whenever I could – that is all.'

'Then you, too, have known sorrow.'

'Yes, sorrow more bitter than death.'

The younger man held out his hand. 'Thank you for telling me this,' he said. 'I can accept favours from you now. I will do as you bid me. My name is Geoffry Milbanke. My mother's name before she married was Dallas. Her father was Squire Dallas of Rowanstone Court, in the Ewas Lacy Valley. She, the only child, was left an orphan when very young, and her money was squandered by her guardians. She married a North Country clergyman, who was poor. He lived until I was 15 years of age, and my mother's life has been one of constant struggle. I had a taste for art, and my mother gave me what chances she could, but I failed to obtain patrons. Almost the last penny we possessed we spent in coming to Ross. My mother once knew some people of the name of Kyrle who lived here, and she thought that perhaps they would give me a helping hand.'

'And have you sought them?' asked the Man of Ross.

'No. I heard that there was but one man of that name in the town, and that he has no taste for art.'

John Kyrle laughed long and loudly.

'Indeed, but they are quite wrong,' he said. 'I am John Kyrle, and I have a most wonderful work of art in progress in my house at the present time. I am forming my coat of arms upon two doors.'

There was good-natured satire in his tone.

'Carving them?' asked Geoffry Milbanke, and for the first time there was animation in his voice.

'Nay, I cannot manage that,' said the Man of Ross. 'I'm perforating the panels – just thrusting hot irons through them in a pattern, d'ye see? They'll be mighty fine, I think.'

Geoffry groaned. 'Are the doors of good oak?' he asked.

'Of a surety – there is naught but oak in my house,' said the Man of Ross, 'but you'll soon see the doors for yourself, and mayhap you will be able to advise me as to how I must go on with them. Now, indeed, I think 'tis strange that I should have found you out, when you had come to Ross to seek me. I do not doubt me but that tonight is the turning point in your life. I am no judge of artistic work myself, but I have a friend in London who is a great artist – Sir Aubrey Miller – he who painted the great picture *Palmam Qui Meruit Ferat*; he shall see thy work and tell thee what he thinks of it. I believe he will judge it kindly. Thou wouldst not have struggled at the one thing all these years, if thou hadst had no gift. I will away now to make ready for you – and we will have a right good Christmas. Tell your mother of the plans meanwhile.'

An hour or two later, a party of four had assembled around the glowing hearthstone in the cosy dining room of Master Kyrle's house – the Man of Ross, his cousin, Mistress Judith Bubb, Geoffry Milbanke, and his mother. Supper was over, and on the polished oak table had been placed wine and fruit. Geoffry's dog lay stretched out before the fire, sighing with

content. The old lady dozed in her high-backed chair.
Mistress Bubb knitted quietly – her eyes never glancing at
her work but fixed upon the huge burning logs which lay
upon the fire-dogs. She was thinking of Christmasses long
since passed, and her heart, which had never had quite enough
to fill it, ached a little with longings unsatisfied. Master
Kyrle and Geoffry talked together in low tones. 'You shall go
to London,' the Man of Ross said, 'and see Sir Aubrey Miller.
Your mother must stay with Mistress Bubb the while.'

'But I have no money, Master Kyrle, and it doth take much
to travel so far.'

'There is a way in which the money can be got,' said Master
Kyrle. 'But thou must not ask questions.'

Later on, when his guests had retired, the Man of Ross took
a lamp in his hand, and going into his own sitting room, once
more unlocked his cabinet. In one of its deepest drawers he
found a small sealed parcel. He broke the seal and disclosed
two small buckles richly encrusted with diamonds. Long years
ago these buckles had been stitched upon a pair of little shoes
and worn at a girl's first dance. They had been given to John
Kyrle to keep in memory of the wearer. He looked at them
now reverently. 'They shall be sold tomorrow,' he murmured.
'She would have wished it.'

Then he locked his cabinet, and turned away with the open
packet in his hand.

The church bells were clanging and clashing as he traversed
the long corridor which led to his bedroom. He paused at a
window and gazed upon the white world without, and some
words from his favourite George Herbert came to his lips:

> The shepherds sing; and shall I silent be,
> My God, no hymne for Thee?
> My soul's a shepherd too: a flock it feeds
> Of thoughts, and words, and deeds.

When Santa Came to Hereford

COLIN COX

*Hereford's Bulmer Railway Centre may seem one of the less
likely places in which to have found Father Christmas
dispensing his seasonal bonhomie and presents, but in fact his
annual visits, as described here by children's author Colin Cox,
were a highspot of the city's festive celebrations for almost a
quarter of a century.*

It all started back in the early 'seventies, when most people
assumed that Father Christmas exclusively travelled by
reindeer-hauled sleigh for his journeying round the country
each year. But here he was in Hereford, at the Bulmer Railway
Centre, with not a sleigh in sight, thoroughly enjoying the
spirit of Christmas in a railway carriage hitched up to a steam
locomotive.

Mind you, it wasn't just an ordinary railway carriage, but a
sort of mobile grotto in which he could feel comfortably at
home, and welcome the hundreds of visitors – young and old
alike – who came to see him.

Presumably he did still have his sleigh, and had parked it
somewhere safe, for he would certainly have needed it later.
His steam train was confined to just a short length of track
and was not going to be much help to him when he was ready

Santa Claus forsakes his sleigh for a steam train in Hereford

to leave on his travels round the rest of the county. But he obviously enjoyed visiting the Bulmer Railway Centre, for until 1992 he had come back every year, making two or three weekend visits in the run-up to Christmas.

His grotto was parked each year at a small halt platform along the line, its steam engine gently hissing to itself as it waited patiently while he welcomed his steady stream of visitors. For them it was a rewarding experience. All the children received a special present which Father Christmas gave them personally, while for their parents there was hot cider punch, cups of tea and mince pies.

Those who wanted a ride on a steam train – which was just about everybody – were not disappointed either, for although Santa's own train was far too busy to be moved, another one puffed up and down the line, giving its Christmastide passengers the chance to enjoy a way of travel which Hereford – like the rest of the country – lost many years ago. And all the while, the gaily decorated railway echoed to the sound of Christmas music, accompanied by the nostalgic huffing and puffing of a real live steam engine hard at work.

Sadly, Father Christmas can look forward no longer to visiting his steam-hauled grotto in Hereford each year. In 1993, just seven months before his planned Christmas arrival, the Bulmer Railway Centre had to close. Father Christmas, like his thousands of annual visitors, can now only look back on the pleasures of almost twenty-five memorable festive seasons. Something he will particularly miss, is one of the regular questions from his younger visitors which he always enjoyed answering: 'No, he didn't have to climb down the chimney of his steam engine!'

Happy Christmas!

On Christmas Day

THOMAS TRAHERNE

*Although Thomas Traherne is now regarded as one of our
major early poets, much of his work was not discovered until
relatively recently – an important part of it in the present
century. He lived from 1637 to 1674, and was born either in
Lugwardine or Hereford – opinions differ about the exact
location. His works include both poetry and prose, and reflect a
mastery of descriptive writing, exemplified here in the sincerity
of six verses from his seasonal poem 'On Christmas Day'.*

Shall dumpish melancholy spoil my joys
While angels sing
And mortals ring
My Lord and Saviour's praise!
Awake from sloth, for that alone destroys,
'Tis sin defiles, 'tis sloth puts out thy joys.
See how they run from place to place,
And seek for ornaments of grace;
Their houses deck'd with sprightly green,
In winter makes a summer seen;
They bays and holly bring
As if 'twere spring!

Shake off thy sloth, my drowsy soul, awake;
With angels sing
Unto thy King,
And pleasant music make;

Thy lute, thy harp, or else thy heart-strings take,
And with thy music let thy sense awake.
See how each one the other calls
To fix his ivy on the walls,
Transplanted there it seems to grow
As if it rooted were below:
Thus He, who is thy King,
Makes winter, spring.

'Tis He that life and spirit doth infuse:
Let everything
The praises sing
Of Christ the King of Jews;
Who makes things green, and with a spring infuse
A season which to see it doth not use:
Old Winter's frost and hoary hair,
With garlands crowned, bays doth wear;
The nipping frost of wrath being gone,
To Him the manger made a throne,
Due praises let us sing,
Winter and spring.

See how their breath doth smoke, and how they haste
His praise to sing
With cherubim;
They scarce a breakfast taste;
But through the streets, lest precious time should waste,
When service doth begin, to church they haste.
And shall not I, Lord, come to Thee,
The beauty of Thy temple see?
Thy name with joy I will confess,
Clad in my Saviour's righteousness;
'Mong all Thy servants sing
To Thee my King.

I all these joys, above my merit, see
By Thee, my King,
To whom I sing,
Entire convey'd to me.
My treasure, Lord, Thou mak'st Thy people be
That I with pleasure might Thy servants see.
Even in their rude external ways
They do set forth my Saviour's praise,
And minister a light to me;
While I by them do hear to Thee
Praises, my Lord and King,
Whole churches ring.

Hark how remoter parishes do sound!
Far off they ring
For Thee, my King,
Even round about the town:
The churches scatter'd over all the ground
Serve for Thy praise, who art with glory crown'd.
This city is an engine great
That makes my pleasure more complete;
The sword, the mace, the magistrate,
To honour Thee attend in state;
The whole assembly sings;
The minster rings.

from

The Box of Delights

JOHN MASEFIELD

*In complete contrast to Ledbury-born John Masefield's two sea
poems reproduced earlier, is this extract from his delightful
children's story* The Box of Delights, *a classic tale of myth
and magic and real-life history and drama, first published in
1935. It is not difficult to detect in it many thinly-veiled
allusions to the city and county of Hereford, and when it was
televised by the BBC, much of the filming was undertaken in
and around Hereford Cathedral. The story recounts the
extraordinary adventures of Kay Harker on his way home for
the Christmas holidays after his first term at school. He had
been given a Box of Delights by a travelling Punch and Judy
man, and this opened up for him a whole new world of magical
powers and exciting characters. On one occasion he found
himself invited to a Christmas party in the Palace of the
Bishop of Tatchester, where an enormous Christmas tree was the
centre of attraction. . . .*

In the midst of this room was the biggest and most glorious
Christmas tree that had ever been seen in Tatchester. It stood in
a monstrous half-barrel full of what looked like real snow stuck

John Masefield, celebrated poet and son of Ledbury

about with holly and mistletoe. Its bigger boughs were decked with the glittering coloured glass globes which Kay so much admired. The lesser boughs were lit with countless coloured electric lights like tropical fruits: ever so much better, Kay thought, than those coloured candles which drip wax everywhere and so often set fire to the tree and to the presents. At the top of this great green fir tree was a globe of red light set about with fiery white rays for the Christmas star.

The boughs were laden with the most exquisite gifts. For the little ones there were whistles, drums, tops of different kinds, whips, trumpets, swords, pop-guns, pistols that fired caps and others which fired corks. There were also many dolls and teddy-bears. For the older boys there were railways with signals and switches and passenger trains and goods trains, some of which went by steam and others by clockwork. There were goods yards with real goods: little boxes, bales and sacks, real cranes by which these could be hoisted, and pumps by which the engines could get water. There were aeroplanes which you could wind up so that they would fly about the room. There were others which you made to fly by pulling a trigger. There were farmyards with cocks and hens which really pecked, and cows which waggled their heads. There were zoos with all sorts of animals, and aquariums with all sorts of fish (in real water which could not splash out).

Then there were all sorts of mechanical toys, of men boxing, or wrestling, or sawing wood, or beating on anvils. When you wound up these, they would box or wrestle or saw or hammer for three or four minutes. Then there were squirts of all kinds and boxes of soldiers with cavalry and cannons, boxes of bricks and Meccano, and all sorts of adventure books and fairy books. For the girls there were needle-boxes with silver thimbles and cases of needles. There were acting sets with costumes of different colours, so that everyone could dress up to act charades. For each girl there were necklaces,

A snowy winter at Ledbury around the turn of the century.
Masefield was born in the town in 1878

bangles and brooches, and each brooch had the girl's name done in brilliants.

There were also boxes of chocolates and candied fruits, and great glass bottles of barley-sugar, raspberry drops, peppermint drops and acid drops. Then for both boys and girls there were toy boats, some with sails, some with clockwork engines, some with steam engines that would make real steam with methylated spirit furnaces. Hanging from the boughs here and there, were white and scarlet stockings all bulging with chocolate creams done up in silver paper.

All round this marvellous tree were wonderful crackers, eighteen inches long. The Bishop made all the children stand in a double rank round the tree, each with one end of a cracker in each hand. The musicians struck up a tune and they danced in the double rank three times round the Christmas tree. Then the

Bishop gave the word, and they pulled the crackers which went off with a bang together, like cannons. And then, inside the crackers, there were the most lovely decorations – real coats of coloured paper that you could put on, with the most splendid hats and necklets like real gold. Then the Bishop's sister and her friends gave each child two presents, and they all played 'Hunt the Slipper' and other merry games.

from

Boy at The Commercial

ALICK ROWE

Herefordshire author and television playwright Alick Rowe lived for much of the first eighteen years of his life in his family's public house – The Commercial – in Hereford. It proved to be a rich catalyst for the experiences and characters he so vividly records in his autobiographical Boy at The Commercial *– from which this colourful account of a memorable boyhood Christmas shortly after the Second World War is taken.*

It would all begin to happen many weeks before. The making of the puddings, of course, was the first sign that Christmas

was not far round some sort of immediate corner, a reality, and the cake came next.

But these were signposts of intent, and the real excitement came sharply with the arrival of Ellsidon's Christmas catalogue. I've never known any book with the same ability to screw expectation six notches up in the pit of the stomach; here was Santa's plenty, if you could afford it – gifts, jokes, decorations. I liked the jokes best. There were the painless 'wifebeaters' of bright folded cardboard which made huge detonations when clapped across the rear of an aunt, indoor fireworks, black paper beetles to float on tea, hinged teaspoons to bend in the middle, soap that turned you black, mock soot, plates of thin metal that resembled broken glass when dropped.

We all went through the catalogue – though none more keenly than I – seeking our different needs and diversions, and when the large impassive box was delivered by the postman, I knew for sure that Christmas was under way.

The decorations of previous years were brought out from Nan's boxroom and repairs were made, the irreparable replaced. I spent hours in the kitchen gumming coloured strips of paper into chains. The secret network of Christmas presents began – Bill slipped me cash for Mum's gift, Mum gave me money for Nan's and Bill's, and so on. The silver threepenny pieces were boiled sterile for the pudding, and I sent my letter to Father Christmas lurching up the chimney on a column of smoke, knowing he didn't exist, and hadn't existed ever since Mum dropped my Christmas banjo down a whole flight of stairs, years ago on Christmas Eve, and was caught red-handed and giggling with her arms full of brightly wrapped boxes.

Only about a week to go, and the pub was transformed into a magic place of vivid papers, cotton wool, holly and strategically placed mistletoe. As ever, we would be fairly full

The successful Hereford writer Alick Rowe who spent many a happy
childhood Christmas at The Commercial

this Christmas. It was Bill's big time: he threw open his house
only once a year, he said, and his guests were welcome to
everything he had. The amazing and beautiful fact was that he
meant it. Bill was like that: no expense spared for his friends and
his family, and when, at his death, people remarked how little he
had left in the way of personal fortune, those of us who knew him
well were in no way surprised and loved his memory the more.

With everything more or less prepared, there was nothing

much to do but enjoy the few days before Christmas. The customers were a cheery lot anyway, but they became noisier and jollier as expectancy grew: I was allowed to release my Ellsidon's jokes on them. Carols began to be sung; more friends than usual were taken into our lounge for drinks; I gave a puppet show and floated about the place in a state of constant euphoria, dead drunk on adult bonhomie. Presents were wrapped and hidden tantalizingly, on top of wardrobes. At last it was Christmas Eve.

The tree came in from the conservatory to be new-rooted in a crisps tin disguised by crêpe paper with a layer of cotton wool snow over sludgy earth from the back garden. The special tree decorations were brought out, and every addition of the well-known, well-loved spangles, tinsel, fairies, nutmegs, lanterns and fragile shining balls produced fresh wonder.

The star, less glittering and spiky than in earlier years, but impossible to replace, topped the highest branch, and finally the coloured lights were entwined and switched on. We all stood back to worship. We were not a religious family: we loved the time and its trappings, the fun, food, drink and each other.

For me, the final tangible proof that it was all under way would be the arrival of Bill's brother, Uncle Rowland, with his wife Tess, and my cousin Carl, from Bishop's Castle. There they were at last, shouting greetings as they came through the bars. Carl was my own age, and as the grown-ups carried gifts, luggage, goose and cake in from the car at the door, we swapped footballing stories. And much later, after numerous visits to the uproarious bars, after carols on the steps from visiting singers with the whole house in deep, contented silence, after more jokes, more games, tipsy parents swept us unprotesting to our different rooms where we were eager to undress and get to bed, knowing we were only hours away from the greatest day of the year.

The night was short but the waiting long. At various times

I would wake to find the room I shared with my mother, on special occasions of celebration or sickness, still empty, with only the hiss and pop of the gas fire to break the dark silence. Then came another wakening, when the warmth of my sleeping mother and the yielding, uneven weights on my probing feet told me everything was all right, and ready. And after that there was little sleep, if any.

The delay as the clock crept round to a respectable seven o'clock was torture. The heaviness on my legs of a load of presents, just out of reach, wound me to fever pitch, and I lay in the warm dark, barely able to support the tension, hoping to communicate the urgency to the sleeping form at my side, and waiting desperately for a grunt or the merest flicker of an eyelid – anything for an excuse: those long minutes would drive me crazy. Could I feign a coughing fit?

Then – *wham*. Mum stirred. I shouted 'Is it time?' and dived for the foot of the bed without waiting for an answer. landing on a beautiful jumble of sharp edges and crinkling paper. The light went on and . . . Oh God, oh God . . . just look. Mum kissed me happy Christmas, but first things first, and that meant the bulging sock on the brass bedstead – one of Bill's for greater capacity. Chocolate, an orange, a small book, sweets, a car, a diary, another car, more chocolate, toy soldiers, a miniature bottle of real port, sweet cigarettes, coloured pencils. The empty sock hit the floor and Mum was grinning up at me as she lit the gas fire.

A series of shouts and greetings from over the corridor, and I'd beaten Carl by a long sock; we hurled greetings back but no time for triumph. Presents waited to be ripped into sight; the flat one first because it was Mum's and I knew it would be something to dress up in – last year it was a bus conductor's kit. This year . . . a thrashing of wrappings . . . and it was a cowboy outfit: hat, belt, guns, sheriff's star and spurs. I screamed my gratitude and tore into the rest as Mum ran through the litany of donors – that's

from Nan and Bill; that one's from Thelma, Lloyd and Butch; Harry Jay's; that's another from me; that's from Les; Bill said you wanted one of those; I can't remember who that's from. There were games and books, a camera from Harry, comics, toys, a tiny cardboard bar counter stocked with tiny non-alcoholic drinks. The crumpled pile of wrapping paper grew at the side of the bed until the orgy was over and I sat, dumb at my good fortune.

The wireless was switched on; carols and bells. I remembered the bit about it being more blessed to give (though I didn't believe it), retrieved Mum's present from behind the chest of drawers and handed it over: a brooch. Then a last check on each tremendous thing and into my clothes. On with my kit too; there would be a sheriff at breakfast.

Tess made toast while Nan poured tea. It was a treat; we never bothered, usually. The day was over its first, best bit. Carl and I bore our armfuls down from the bedrooms into the Commercial Room where there was space to play. But the morning's fun would be in the bars and by mid-day we were there, to greet Harry and Doug, to cram mince pies into our mouths, to set up drinks for Phil. I rushed for my camera from Harry and used half a roll of film snapping tipsy customers and indulgent family.

By two the lounge was made ready for Christmas dinner. The best tablecloths stretched immaculately over the table, lengthened to its furthest extent and carrying a gleaming array of cutlery, cruets, glasses, plates. In the sweating kitchen, Nan was coping with the cooking on two gas cookers beneath limp paper chains. Puddings were boiling, the turkey roasting, gravy simmering, and trayloads of serving dishes standing ready as we all waited for the last customers to leave.

Some of them were to join us. Harry tapped at the kitchen door, bringing drinks for the cooks and news that the bars were almost empty. Les – next year to become my stepfather – could be heard carrying crates of empties down to the cellar.

Jackie was with us this year, a likeable, lonely lady, with a limp and man's deep voice; she came pressing through to offer help, but it was all running to time. We would sit down about a dozen strong. Then Bill came in to stir everyone up; was nobody doing anything but him? A shocked melodramatic astonishment at the array of food and dishes. What was all this? He'd said bread and cheese this year!

Two courses, but massive, with champagne on the table for anyone who wanted it and glasses ready for varying tastes. Turkey, potatoes, sprouts, stuffing, gravy and bread sauce: plates went to and fro, filling, refilling; dishes were emptied and replenished. We were all hungry and Nan was a splendid cook.

The pudding appeared, vast, dark, secret, and crammed with silver threepenny bits. Over it went half a bottle of brandy and out went the lights while Bill touched a match to

A glance back to an earlier Christmas in Hereford: the scene at High Town in 1897

the pool of spirit. We cheered the eerie blue flame. The lights went back on and Nan dished the pudding out, swamping it with sharp, sweet brandy sauce. Harry had a coin; a cheer. Another – Tess this time. Carl and I savaged our portions in frantic rummaging and – yes, but . . . a ten shilling note? I held it up, bemused, to more cheers and Bill's wink. Uncle Rowland demanded a coin and Nan said she'd seen one in his helping when she dished it out. Uncle Rowland's eyes boggled; he clutched his throat; we shrieked. He poured champagne down his throat and began to choke; we shrieked again. He coughed into his handkerchief and glared astonished, then smiled as he wonderingly held up the coin. It was a good act.

Mince pies for anyone? Well, maybe. Then, finally, toasts. Bill stood, solemn and sincere, raising his glass and wishing all beneath his roof a very happy Christmas – a moving moment for us all, sensing the strong bonds of family. Then the second toast: absent friends. This was quieter and there was silence as we recalled Uncle Cecil, brother to Bill and Rowland, who had died during the year, and Thelma, five thousand miles away in West Virginia, her first Christmas from home. Round the room eyes filled. Then Harry stood up shyly to thank Nan and Bill for their hospitality on behalf of the guests, and to wish us compliments of the season. We blinked away our emotion and forced back the party mood, slow but gathering: we had guests and would not involve them with private griefs. We staggered from the table. The second highlight of the day was over.

Now, although the routine of the day was attended to – the women tackled the enormous pile of washing-up, there was Christmas cake and tea afterwards – things remained in a state of suspension until the bars were opened at seven, and attention turned to the final miracle of Christmas Day, Bill's party in The Commercial Room.

In the pre-war days when The Commercial was a hotel, this had been the dining room; it had a speaking tube which ran down to the passage outside the kitchen. The floor was high-class rubber, a mysterious purchase from a liner at Southampton. It was a long room, and one wall was of glass sections interspersed with glass doors which led out on to a balcony overlooking Commercial Road. Two-thirds of the way down the room, a heavy blue velvet curtain could be drawn across and this made a natural theatre for all sorts of festivities.

Nan, Mum, Tess and a band of helpers ran back and forth from the kitchen, setting the table in the room with cold turkey and other meats, bread and cheese, pickles, mince pies and cake. Les and Rowland, with other guests, began to haul crates of beer, whisky, gin and Guinness to one end of the room. A wide range of glasses stood ready. The Commercial Room, by ten, looked superb. Carl and I were no longer sent early to bed, our feeding bottles unfairly drugged with hot milk and gin, but were likely to be removed when we began to falter, or if the party became too boisterous. It usually lasted well into Boxing Day morning, till four or five, and it was not until we were teenagers that we managed to see it out, or share officially in the drinking.

The pub closes at ten but there is work for everybody, guests and all, before the party can take place. At last, when the house is ready for the morning, the rituals of the night begin. Bill insists, this year as every year, that all non-family must leave the premises as customers and return as friends, and solemnly everyone has been shown out and wished goodnight, to wander a while along Commercial Road before turning back to be welcomed by Nan and Bill. They are urged upstairs, until thirty, maybe forty, of us are helping ourselves to drinks and singing carols, led by Mum at the piano.

The first hour is all singing and dancing; the popular songs of the time rise with the smoke and heat, quiet and contented.

At midnight, the second ritual has to be run through. A large jug is filled with beer and we all move down to the steps of The Commercial to sing Christmas Day out. We fill the porch and spill on to the pavement, carolling, while smiling passers-by are wished goodnight and fed with beer if they so wish.

When Nan has had enough of the December air, she and most of the women file back upstairs, but the men take their jug and songs a hundred yards down the road to the public lavatory on the corner by the station and give their performance all over again.

From the porch or the balcony we hear the tipsy strains floating back, and laugh at the lovely nonsense of it all, pointing out the amazement of people still in the streets and showing hilarious anxiety at the occasional patrolling policeman, who will certainly be regaled with the jug when he meets the serenaders on their return journey.

And after all this, the party really takes off . . .

And so, the festivities progress, becoming ever noisier and smokier. There are games to be played and more carols to be sung, before, inevitably, they give way to a succession of favourite bawdy songs. Eventually, in the early hours of Boxing Day morning, Alick and Carl are persuaded to bid the revellers goodnight and they 'creep upstairs, unwashed, washed out, to stagger into pyjamas'. For them, another Christmas at The Commercial is over.

The 'Holy Thorns' of Wye

HAL BETHELL

The legend of the Holy Thorn is an ancient one, persisting right up to the present day and taking on a special significance each Christmastime. Herefordshire can trace more associations with the story than any other county, as writer Hal Bethell discovered when he wrote this account in 1988.

There is an ancient legend, passed down from father to son, connecting Herefordshire with the Holy Land of Biblical times. One solitary fragment of living evidence may bear the story out.

Tradition tells us that Christianity was brought to Britain by Joseph of Aramathea, the disciple who laid the body of Jesus in the tomb. The story goes on to relate how Joseph travelled with a hawthorn staff, cut from the tree that provided the crown of thorns.

Coming ashore at Avalon (the modern Glastonbury in Somerset), then an island, Joseph drove the stake into the ground, perhaps as a tent-pole or to claim territory. It immediately took root, and thereafter bloomed each year on old Christmas Eve, 5 January.

Henry VIII, in 1537, hearing news of this curious thorn, sent an emissary to investigate. From him he received 'two flowers wrapped in black sarsnet' from the bush 'that at the very hour when Christ was born, will spring and burgeon and bear blossom'.

However, the courtier's report, the first written record of the so-called Holy Thorn, made no mention at all of Joseph. He did not come into the story by name for well over a hundred years, when it was put about that he had planted the mysterious thorn. Not until 1716 – in a century which savoured its 'wondrous tales' – did the version begin to circulate that the thorn had sprouted from Joseph's miraculous staff. Even then it was a tap-room tale told to a traveller by an inn-keeper.

Teasing fact from fiction in this tanglewood tale is difficult, but it is known that many possible descendants of the Holy Thorn have grown in Herefordshire – more than in any other county.

In 1752, the calendar was changed and Christmas edged back to 25 December, causing great resentment. Many rejected the new Christmas Day, saying that the Holy Thorns were not in bloom, and old Christmas Day was commonly celebrated in the county well into the nineteenth century.

Francis Kilvert, Vicar of Bredwardine, wrote in 1878: 'I went to the little farmhouse at Dolfach to see the Holy Thorn there in blossom. The tree (a graft from the old Holy Thorn at Tibberton now cut down) bloomed on old Christmas Eve and there were fifteen people watching round the tree to see it blow at midnight.'

In the following year, one of the coldest on record, Kilvert wrote: 'Last night, the slip of the Holy Thorn which John Parry of Dolfach grafted for me last spring in the vicarage lower garden, blossomed in an intense frost.' As is the case with so many of Herefordshire's Holy Thorns, this tree no longer exists.

The 'holy thorn' breaks into bloom on old Christmas Eve

The only Herefordshire thorn associated with a Christian shrine, grew at Wormsley by the Priory, not far from the Grange. In Victorian days, Weobley folk made up parties to witness the blow and carry sprigs of blossom home. Ella Leather, the county folklorist, wrote of her visit to Wormsley in 1898: 'About forty people were there, and it was quite dark and the blossom could be seen by candlelight. It was probably the warmth of the candles which made some of the little white buds seem to expand.'

At one time, the event was advertised in the local paper, and torchlight parties were led to see the hilltop tree. Sadly, this thorn was killed off in the bitter winter of 1947/8.

Possibly the best-known Holy Thorn in the county was at Orcop. In 1949, the local paper reported nearly two hundred people congregating by bicycle, car and coach to see the blossom appear on old Christmas Eve. The Orcop thorn continued to attract visitors until one year high winds destroyed it.

At Rowlstone a Holy Thorn was seen in 'fair blossom' at midnight on Twelfth Night in 1898. At the turn of the century, according to Ella Leather, the visitors who turned out to see this thorn blow in the garden of Kingstone Grange were regaled with cider.

All these Holy Thorns died of natural causes, but two of long ago were destroyed by man's hand. At Clehonger, a farmer took fright when his axe blows were said to have produced a flow of blood from the tree. Another farmer, in Acton Beauchamp, was so incensed by trespassing sightseers, that he cut his thorn down. His action almost cost him 'an arm and a leg', for both were broken within the year, and in addition, his farmhouse was gutted by fire.

In the past, other Holy Thorns have grown at Dorstone, Colwall, Stoke Edith, Staunton-on-Wye, and in a garden hedge at Alfrick, over the border in Worcestershire.

Probably the only Holy Thorn left alive today in Herefordshire is at Kingsthorne. It is still occasionally visited on old Christmas Eve by small groups of thorn-watchers. A Mr Haggatt of Hereford records going to see it in 1949 'in a sceptical frame of mind, just to make certain that the whole thing was an old wives' tale'. He could scarcely believe the evidence of his own eyes when he saw the buds actually opening.

But why have there been so many Holy Thorns in Herefordshire? Various theories provide clues to the answer. Iron Age people, in their drive westward, travelled up the Severn and Wye into what is now Herefordshire. The thorns may well have been planted by them as pagan symbols of creation and rebirth.

On the other hand, as this particular thorn appears originally to have been a Levantine plant, the variety may indeed have been introduced into this country by Joseph of Aramathea. It is possible that he journeyed up the Wye, preaching Christianity and planting thorn bushes as he went. Perhaps cuttings from the original Holy Thorn were later brought into the area by monks from Glastonbury, or by pilgrims returning from the Holy Land.

Whoever brought Herefordshire its Holy Thorns must have introduced them as entire plants or understood the principles of grafting, for the species does not breed true. Its seedlings revert to the common hawthorn.

This fact alone, quite apart from the story's historical interest, provides compelling reason for slips to be taken from the curious Kingsthorne tree before it, too, dies. Only in this way can the last living evidence of the Holy Thorn tradition in Herefordshire be preserved.

from

Fancies and Fragments

FREDERICK HOSKYNS MATTHEWS

*As the author made clear, this little anthology of poetry, first
published in 1878, was compiled 'with special reference to the
locality of Hereford'. One such 'special reference' is the delightfully
descriptive poem reproduced here, entitled 'A Winter Piece'.*

Old Winter at last with his bleak biting blast
The landscape has stript of its sheen;
Upon Wye's fair flood, and o'er Rotherwas wood
His influence fatal is seen.

He has rifled those bowers of their fruits and their flowers,
And spread desolation and death;
Of what Autumn had left those banks are bereft
By his pitiless pestilent breath.

His looks are most bitter, and he makes a sad litter,
Strews his spoils like a woodman around;
He has need of a score of stout workmen and more
His rubbish to clear from the ground.

'Old winter at last with his bleak biting blast . . .' This early
photograph, taken around the turn of the century, shows snow
being cleared from Hereford's old Wye Bridge

A Herefordshire Christmas

His air is so freezing he sets us all sneezing,
And makes e'en the blithest look blue;
He chills ev'ry fountain, and compels yon black mountain
To wear quite an opposite hue.

Can this be the land where with Classic in hand
We saunter'd beside the bright stream,
Where the thrush's shrill voice bade the light heart
   rejoice,
And all smil'd as a Summer night's dream?

But let us be merry though old Aconbury
Shake his wild hoary locks at our mirth,
Over lorn Ladylift though the snow-storms they drift,
The yule log shall blaze high on our hearth.

Round Robin Hood's butts though the wind keen it cuts,
For good cheer it but sharpens our zest;
Though from Dinmore to Dinedor the prospect's not
   kinder,
Where's the view like an old English feast?

If our mails are all stopping, and our mercuries dropping,
We can wait for the news from afar,
And with stout or stire toasting, and with Christmas
   cakes roasting,
We'll bring Fahrenheit fast up to par.

Then as music and dancing our revels enhancing
Shall banish the foul fiend dull Care,
Let us think of the labours of our poor shiv'ring
   neighbours,
And let them our warm feelings share.

Where Has All the Ritual Gone?

JOHN NORTON

In earlier pages, some of Herefordshire's traditional Christmas customs – many of which have now died out – are described in extracts from a paper read in 1877 to the Woolhope Club by the Reverend James Davies. In 1990, writer and journalist John Norton carried out a study of these and other ancient rites of the festive season. He based much of his research on the writings of the county's celebrated folklorist Ella Mary Leather, whose book The Folklore of Herefordshire, *published in 1912, is still regarded by many as the definitive work on the subject.*

Christmas, wrote a contributor to *The Hereford Times* in the 1950s, is not what it used to be. It never was, he added, quoting the famous retort from *Punch*.

In the 1990s it's a sentiment which has an even truer ring about it. Television, rampant commercialism, relative affluence and an increasing degree of cynicism, have all contributed to changing the character of what we still like to call 'the traditional Christmas', even if there are many who don't have the faintest idea of what the expression really means.

Some may well argue that traditions evolve, and that those which die out are replaced by others, dictated by changing social circumstances. Thus, in future years, the glitzy seasonal

seduction now offered by the television set, may well be seen as one of the principal components of 'the traditional Christmas', in the same way as charades or the game of snapdragon were inseparable from any celebrations worth their name a century ago.

But despite everything, there are, of course, a few of the old traditions which do survive, to ensure that our modern Christmases still retain at least some of the elements which have always made this particular festival something rather special. We still sing carols, and feast as lustily as ever; we still decorate our homes and exchange greetings and presents; and there are those who still recognise the essential meaning of the occasion by attending church, even if more than a few of them don't go anywhere near a place of worship for the rest of the year. And, of course, Father Christmas is still eagerly anticipated by the younger generation – or most of them – despite the inconvenient fact that his traditional method of entry into many of their bedrooms has now disappeared in this age of central heating and chimneyless houses.

In times past though, when life, by modern standards, was a good deal less sophisticated and was lived at a more sedate pace, the Christmas period was marked by numerous curious and colourful customs, many of them associated with day-to-day life on the land and its overriding influence on the very existence of many people.

In Herefordshire's cider orchards, for instance, the ancient custom of wassailing was a highspot of the festive season. Its traditional purpose was to ensure a good crop of apples in the following autumn, and the ritual, although embodying a number of basic elements, differed in detail from area to area. It was usually held on New Year's Eve or New Year's Night, or occasionally on the eve of Old Christmas Day, 5 January. This reflected the deeply held conviction – which persisted in Herefordshire longer than in most counties – that the 'real'

Christmas Day was on 6 January and that the adjustment of the calendar in 1752 should be ignored.

The wassailers would select a number of trees in the orchard, dancing round them as they sang one of the traditional wassail songs:

> Here's to thee, old apple tree,
> Whence thou may'st bud
> And whence thou may'st blow,
> And whence thou may'st
> Bear apples enow;
> Hats full and caps full,
> Bushels full and sacks full,
> And my pockets full too.

At the same time they would create a deafening noise by banging together metal tools and implements, or hitting the trees with stakes, in order to scare away any evil spirits which may be lurking around. This cacophonous performance was also intended, in some areas, to wake up the god of the orchard from his winter slumber, so that he could exert a benevolent influence on the proceedings. Other more recent versions of the custom mention the firing of guns, to achieve the same purpose.

The wassailers always took with them a good supply of cider, not only for their own refreshment but for aiding the fertility of the trees by applying it to the branches or roots. They would also leave an offering of food for the birds – robins in particular, as they were believed to bring good luck – and this would take the form of crumbs with a little salt, or something more substantial like pieces of toast soaked in cider.

This quaint tradition was frequently accompanied by an even more bizarre custom known as 'Burning the Bush', the purpose again being to ensure a good harvest. It was not only

enacted in the apple orchards, but also in the newly-sown cornfields, and as with wassailing, there are various versions on record.

One such version refers to the 'bush' being a piece of hawthorn with its ends bent inwards and twisted together to form a rough globular shape. This was said by some to

The ancient 'Burning the Bush' ceremony involved a small branch cut from a hawthorn bush and twisted into the shape shown here. This example came from a farm at Pembridge in 1897, and can still be seen today in Hereford Museum

represent Christ's crown of thorns, and by others to match the shape of the reawakening sun. The bush would be burned with great ceremony on a fire of blazing straw in the middle of the cornfield, and a second newly-made bush would be passed through the smoke and singed. This would then be kept in the farmhouse until the following year, when it too would be burned and the ceremony repeated.

Another version of the ritual describes each farmhand taking a wisp of blazing straw – or one person taking the burning bush itself – and trying to run with it over thirteen ridges of sown corn before it went out. If they succeeded, a good harvest was sure to follow.

Yet another account of the burning bush ceremony mentions the lighting of thirteen fires in a circle – either in a cornfield or orchard – representing Christ (or occasionally the Virgin Mary) and the twelve apostles. The fire allocated to Judas was extinguished, leaving twelve burning, and in the centre the bush was ignited to signify the rekindling of the sun and thus ensure a bounteous crop in the fullness of time.

In recent years, these ancient rural customs of wassailing and burning the bush, have been revived by the Leominster Morris Men, bringing a strange touch of incongruity to the modern orchards of today's cider producers, but at the same time providing a fascinating reminder of a past way of life.

A curious ritual which would often follow the wassailing and bush-burning, involved a specially made cake with a hole in the centre. The party of revellers would adjourn to the cattle shed, where mugs of cider would be raised and each of the resident oxen suitably toasted:

> Fill your cups my merry men all,
> For here's the best ox in the stall,
> Oh, he is the best ox, of that there's no mistake,
> And so let us crown him with the Twelfth cake.

Then the cake with the hole would be placed on one of the horns of the first ox, and the beast goaded, either with a stick or by having cider thrown in its face. This, not surprisingly, caused the unfortunate beast to toss its head, throwing the cake into the air. Depending on where the cake fell – in front of the ox or behind – it became the property either of the farm bailiff or of the lowest servant. On some farms, the way the cake fell to the ground would determine either a good or bad harvest in the ensuing year.

Another old Herefordshire Christmas custom, and one which would not go down very well in these days of equality of the sexes, deemed that it was extremely unlucky for a woman to be the first to enter a house on Christmas Day, unless she had slept there on the previous night. This would have exempted the farmer's wife who, in any case, would be busy in the farm kitchen preparing the Christmas food. If she was sensible, she would already have ensured future good luck by paying a dark-haired man to be the first person to enter the front door of her house on Christmas Day, making certain he visited each room in turn before departing through the back door.

The festive season was also enlivened by house-to-house visits by the wassailers – presumably when they were not otherwise engaged in singing and dancing and lighting fires in the orchards. They would sing carols and Christmas songs, and proffer a large wassail bowl made of maple wood, which was topped up at each house with ale or a libation of hot cider, gin, nutmeg and sugar.

In the last century it was usual for most of the larger Herefordshire farmhouses to have a staff of servants, and they were generally allowed to stay up to welcome in the New Year. At midnight they would take part in yet another of the county's now long-gone seasonal customs – collecting the 'cream of the well'. This was the first water drawn from the well in the New Year, and it was thought to possess special

qualities bestowing beauty and good luck on those who washed in it or drank it. Like all good servants, they took none of these benefits for themselves, but ensured that the water went straight to their mistresses who gave them a coin for their trouble.

New Year's Day was also a time for a delightful custom known as New Year Gifting, which persisted throughout

A decorated apple supported on three wooden legs was often used as a gift in the old Herefordshire custom known as New Year Gifting

117

Herefordshire for much of the last century. The countryfolk, and children too, would call at the more wealthy houses offering small 'lucky' ornaments in exchange for gifts. These ornaments usually consisted of an apple or orange mounted on three wooden legs and decorated with various nuts and sprigs of box and holly, highlighted with gold or silver glitter. They would adorn houses for as long as they lasted – which, one imagines, could not have been very long – although the good luck they were supposed to guarantee, would endure the whole year through.

Considering all the superstitions and customs which once had to be observed, it's tempting to wonder if our forebears had much time left in which to do anything else over the Christmas period. It was unlucky, for instance, to borrow fire at Christmas – a very necessary operation before the invention of matches – unless a small gift was given in return.

It was no less unlucky to receive new shoes or anything made of untanned leather during Christmas week, or to bring decorative greenery into the house before Christmas Eve. And it was asking for trouble if elder was burned in the Christmas hearth. The traditional yule log, on the other hand, was a symbol of security and wellbeing, but it was never allowed to be entirely consumed by the fire. A small piece had to be very carefully preserved until the following Christmas, as a precaution against fire and lightning. Accompanying it would be a sprig of mistletoe, which gave additional all-the-year-round protection against ill luck.

It might all sound exceedingly quaint by comparison with our modern Christmas festivities, but in the days when rural communities were virtually self-contained, with few outside influences, folklore played an important role in people's daily existence. This was particularly so at Christmastime, when the promise of a new year and the banishing of the cold, dark days of winter, had a profound effect on the lives of countryfolk. In Herefordshire, they certainly made the most of it.

A Herefordshire Christmas

In the foregoing chapter, John Norton refers to the revival of the old wassailing custom by the Leominster Morris Men. This is the subject of a chapter to be found in later pages.

Enjoying games and skating on the ice has always been a popular pastime in our severest winters. This was the scene on the Wye at Hereford in the winter of 1892

from

Cider for all Seasons

MARY BERRY

Cider and Herefordshire are almost synonymous, and although most people probably think of it mainly as a refreshing beverage in its own right, it also has a special significance in the context of cooking. It can, in fact, enhance a wide range of dishes, as Mary Berry's Cider for all Seasons *proves, and her Christmas recipes are no exception. The following examples all depend on the addition of Herefordshire cider for their festive excellence.*

MINCEMEAT
(Makes about 5 lbs)

Mincemeat made with cider has a lovely rich flavour.

1½ lbs (675 g) stoned raisins
½ lb (225 g) cooking apples
4 ozs (100 g) candied peel
12 ozs (325 g) currants
8 ozs (225 g) sultanas
6 ozs (175 g) shredded suet
½ level teaspoon mixed spice
2 lemons

1 lb (450 g) soft brown sugar
6 tablespoons (90 ml) extra-dry cider such as
   Bulmer's No 7

Finely chop or mince the raisins and peel. Peel, core and
mince or chop the apples. Place in a large bowl with the other
fruit, suet and spice.

Grate the rind and squeeze the juice from the lemons. Add
to the fruit with the sugar and cider. Mix well.

Cover the bowl and leave to stand overnight. Next day turn
into clean jars, cover and label.

A FIRST-RATE PLUM PUDDING

This old-fashioned rich Christmas pudding improves with
keeping. Boil it for at least 10 hours in total, and it will be a
rich golden brown. Remember to keep the water topped up
during cooking, especially on Christmas morning when there
are lots of other things on your mind.

8 ozs (225 g) self-raising flour
1 level teaspoon (5 ml) mixed spice
$\frac{1}{2}$ level teaspoon grated nutmeg
1 level teaspoon (5 ml) salt
12 ozs (325 g) currants
12 ozs (325 g) sultanas
12 ozs (325 g) stoned raisins
12 ozs (325 g) fresh white breadcrumbs
12 ozs (325 g) suet, finely chopped
4 ozs (100 g) candied peel, finely chopped
2 ozs (50 g) almonds, blanched and chopped
1 cooking apple, peeled, cored and grated
Grated rind and juice of 1 orange
1 lb (450 g) soft brown sugar
6 eggs, beaten

'A first-rate plum pudding . . .'

¹/₄ pint (150 ml) extra-dry cider such as
  Bulmer's No 7

Grease two 2¹/₂-pint pudding basins. Sift together the flour, mixed spice, nutmeg and salt.

Put the dried fruit into a bowl with the breadcrumbs, suet, peel, almonds, grated apple, orange rind and juice. Stir in the spiced flour and sugar. Finally add the eggs and cider. Stir the mixture well, then turn into the basins.

Cover the tops with greaseproof paper and a foil lid, and let the puddings simmer gently for about 7 hours. Lift them out of the pan, leaving the foil and greaseproof paper in place. Cool and store the puddings.

Simmer for a further 3 hours before serving.

HEREFORDSHIRE CIDER CAKE

A spicy cake that the family will love.

    1 orange
    Sweet cider, such as Woodpecker
    4 ozs (100 g) margarine
    6 ozs (175 g) caster sugar
    2 eggs
    8 ozs (225 g) self-raising flour
    ½ level teaspoon mixed spice
    ½ level teaspoon cinnamon
    8 ozs (225 g) currants

Cider will enhance any Christmas dinner

Heat the oven to 350 °F (180 °C), Mark 4. Line and grease the base and sides of a 7-inch cake tin.

Grate the rind from the orange and squeeze out the juice. Make juice up to ¼ pint with cider.

Cream the margarine and sugar in a bowl with the orange rind until light and fluffy. Beat in the eggs one at a time.

Sift the flour and spices together. Stir into the mixture with the currants and cider until mixed to a dropping consistency.

Turn into the tin, smooth the top and bake in the oven for about 1 hour or until the cake feels firm to the touch and a warmed skewer inserted in the centre comes out clean. Leave cake to cool in the tin for about 10 minutes before turning it out. Remove the paper and leave to finish cooling on a wire rack.

Following her recipes for Christmas fare, Mary Berry adds for good measure this anonymous nineteenth-century quatrain extolling the virtues of cider as a drink:

> Good cider 'tis a drink divine,
> Better by far than all your wine,
> Good in grief, good in joy,
> Good for maid, man and boy.

The Boy Bishops of Hereford

HOWARD BROWNE

*The origins of the Boy Bishop ceremony can be traced back
many centuries, and Hereford Cathedral was among the first to
be associated with its deep-rooted traditions. In this account the
Midland writer, Howard Browne, describes its historical
context and its significance in the twentieth century as one of
Hereford's more colourful Christmastide customs.*

Every December, Hereford Cathedral is the imposing setting
for one of the most appealing of traditions in the life of the
Church. This is the appointment of the Boy Bishop, or Bishop
of the Innocents, and its association with English cathedrals
can be traced back as far as the thirteenth century. Hereford
was, in fact, one of the first cathedrals to practise the custom.

Each year's Boy Bishop is a cathedral chorister and a pupil
of Hereford Cathedral School, and nowadays he is elected by
the Chapter, in collaboration with the cathedral organist and
choirmaster. It is not an appointment which can be treated
lightly, as it carries numerous responsibilities, particularly
over the Christmas period, and the selected boy must have a
proven record which fits him for his exalted role.

On the face of it, the custom may seem a strange one, and

125

its origins go back long before it first appeared on the cathedral calendar. It is thought to have its roots in the Roman festival known as Saturnalia, when strange reversals of role took place – commoners became 'kings', servants became masters, and ordinary people, for an all too brief period, took on the identities of lords and ladies and other aristocratic personalities.

Rather than ostracise this unlikely upside-down world, the Christian church decided to adapt it for its own ends and gave it new meaning. What better way of perpetuating the old rituals than by allowing cathedral choristers to provide their own bishop?

In the early days, it was the choristers themselves who elected one of their number to hold the coveted role. The election traditionally took place on 6 December, St Nicholas's Day. This was an appropriate date in the calendar, as St Nicholas is the patron saint of schoolboys. It was he, of course, according to legend, who brought back to life the bodies of three murdered boys who had been cut up and pickled by an unscrupulous innkeeper with the intention of passing them off as salted pork.

Having been elected, the Boy Bishop would assume his duties on 27 December, the day before the Festival of the Holy Innocents when the Biblical child martyrs are remembered.

Clothed in fine vestments for the installation service, the young Bishop with 'a mitre well-garnished with pearls and precious stones' – according to fifteenth-century records – and attended by his boy canons, would lead the procession to the top of the chancel steps. There he received the real Bishop's blessing before taking his place on the throne, while the Bishop himself took a more humble seat in the sanctuary, thus acknowledging the passage in the Magnificat which speaks of 'putting down the mighty from their seat'.

The origins of Hereford Cathedral's Boy Bishop custom can be traced back at least to the thirteenth century. In 1991, the Boy Bishop was cathedral chorister Tim Sarson

In this way the Christian Church could be seen to turn the old pagan rite into a lesson in humility, which was completed by the new Boy Bishop giving his blessing to the congregation.

On the following day the Boy Bishop preached a sermon and received the congregation's offerings. In theory he was allowed to keep the money 'for his own proper uses', although in practice the cathedral authorities would apply it to more worthy causes like the education of the choristers.

The next duty of the Boy Bishop and his retinue was to visit local parishes before finally returning for a lavish feast. One such feast evidently included twelve chickens, eight woodcocks, one plover and two ducks, as well as copious quantities of veal and mutton. This is one aspect of the proceedings which the Boy Bishops of modern times no doubt wish had been retained.

But this whole splendid ritual was doomed to come to an end at the time of the Reformation, when Henry VIII condemned 'the superstitions and childish observances' associated with various saints, including St Nicholas and the Holy Innocents, in his proclamation of 1541: 'Children be strangelie decked and apparayled to counterfeit priestes and bishoppes . . . blessing the people and gatheryng money, and boyes do sing masse and preache in the pulpitt.'

So by the time Elizabeth I was on the throne, the old custom was finally abolished and was not revived again at Hereford until relatively recently, although on a less elaborate scale. It still retains much of its original significance, and the real Bishop – like his earlier counterparts – continues to observe the words of the Magnificat by sitting in a more lowly seat than the young newcomer during the traditional ceremony.

The Boy Bishop is now involved in such occasions as the main carol services in both the cathedral and the cathedral school, while the installation service itself is a ceremonial act

Hereford was one of the first English cathedrals to introduce the
Boy Bishop ceremony. The ancient building is seen here above the
frozen Wye during a wintry festive season towards the end of the
last century

of worship, conducted with due decorum. The preaching of a
short sermon is still one of the Boy Bishop's main official
duties, and the holder of the office always rises to the occasion
thanks largely to his training as a cathedral chorister and to
his presence and personality which were among the
prerequisites when he was chosen. It is these important factors
which also give him the ability to process round the cathedral
in a suitably dignified manner, and generally to conduct
himself in a way befitting his role.

But all too soon the Boy Bishop's short-lived authority reverts again to the Bishop – until the following year when the ancient and endearing custom is repeated once again.

To the cynics it may all appear as a somewhat irrelevant anachronism in the late twentieth century, but to the traditionalists it is a splendid perpetuation of an ancient and meaningful custom which provides an eloquent annual reminder that within the Church, as in other institutions which depend upon the trappings of authority and status, there is indeed virtue in humility.

Hereford Carol

TRADITIONAL

In previous pages there are examples of some rare Christmas carols collected in Herefordshire early this century by Ella Mary Leather and Ralph Vaughan Williams. The carol that follows is from the same collection, where it appears as 'The Angel Gabriel', but it was singled out for inclusion in that worthy tome The Oxford Book of Carols, *in which it is given the title 'Hereford Carol'. An appended note informs readers that the words were collated from various sources, including a Mr Hirons of Dilwyn and a ballad sheet originally published by R. Elliot of Hereford.*

THE ANGEL GABRIEL

Come all you faithful Christians
That dwell here on earth,
Come celebrate the morning
Of our dear Saviour's birth.
This is the happy morning,
This is the blesséd morn,
To save our souls from ruin,
The Son of God was born.

Behold the Angel Gabriel,
In scripture it is said,
Did with his holy message
Come to the Virgin maid:

A Christmas card scene near the village of Ocle Pychard

'Hail blest among all women!'
He thus did greet her then,
'Lo, thou shalt be the mother
Of the Saviour of all men.'

Her time being accomplished,
She came to Bethlehem,
And then was safe delivered
Of the Saviour of all men.
No princely pomp attended Him,
His honours were but small;
A manger was His cradle
His bed an ox's stall.

Now to Him that is ascended
Let all our praises be;
May we His steps then follow,
And He our pattern be;
So when our lives are ended,
We all may hear Him call,
'Come souls, receive the kingdom,
Preparèd for you all.'

Christmas with the Savages

MARY CLIVE

*The Herefordshire authoress Lady Mary Clive, daughter of the
fifth Earl of Longford, who lives with her son George on the
family estate at Whitfield near Hereford, drew on her own
childhood memories when she wrote* Christmas with the
Savages. *It is a charming blend of fact and fiction, and
evocatively reflects the life-style with which, in her younger days,
she was so familiar. This was a time when most families of
similar status had their staff of governess and nursery maids, and
a retinue of upstairs and downstairs servants. Although the
characters are fictitious, they are mostly based on members of her
own Pakenham family and her childhood friends. The story
revolves round a Christmas in the early years of the century when,
due to her father's illness, 'Evelyn' (Mary Pakenham, now Lady
Mary Clive, the authoress) was taken from her London home to
spend the festive season in the country at 'Tamerlane Hall', with
the unpredictable children of the Savage family. In this extract,
she describes the delights and excitements of Christmas Day itself.*

I did really mean to lie awake till Father Christmas came, so
as to settle once and for all who he was. But the room was

The Pakenham children. Left to right: Mary (now Lady Mary Clive),
Edward (sixth Earl of Longford), Pansy (Lady Pansy Lamb), and
Francis (seventh Earl of Longford)

pitch dark except for a strip of light under the door, and it was very difficult to keep my eyes open . . .

Presently I noticed that the crack of light wasn't there any more, and as I lay in the dark I became aware of a strong smell of oranges. Vaguely I wondered where the smell was coming from and then, with a start, I asked myself, could it be coming from my stocking?

Regardless of the cold, I pushed back the bedclothes and crawled to the end of my bed, and my hand met something that was woolly, hard and sharp. Nothing else in the world feels quite like a well-stuffed stocking.

My hand followed the bumps and jags up to the top, and there the woolliness ended and I could feel something which, in the darkness, I mistook for the top of an umbrella – it afterwards turned out to be a book. With a sigh of relief I nipped back under the bedclothes thinking, 'The magic has worked yet once again. He has come.'

We had been told not to get up till half-past-six, and Rosamund had promised to call me so that we could all unpack together. I wondered what the time was, and at that moment the stable clock obligingly struck. I counted fourteen, which seemed strange and exciting, but on thinking it over I decided that I must have added in the chimes and that it was really six. To have to wait for half an hour was almost unbearable, but there seemed nothing else to be done, especially as I had no matches. I tried to lie still but the stocking seemed to pull me towards it, and every few minutes I was down at the end of my bed feeling to make sure that there was no mistake.

At last the stable clock struck half-past and my door was flung open by Rosamund. She was carrying a candle and her hair was in three pigtails tied up with rags.

'Happy Christmas!' she shouted in a voice loud enough to wake the whole of Tamerlane. 'Happy Christmas! Happy Christmas!'

In an instant I was up and had unpinned my stocking which suddenly became so heavy that I dropped it on the floor. I then saw that there were things on the chair as well. I tried not to look to see what they were as I grabbed the lot, and then had to lay them down again as I put on my dressing-gown.

When I got to Rosamund's room I found the other children were already there.

'Two candles aren't enough,' said Lionel, 'and Minnie says that three are very unlucky. Fetch all your candles, Evelyn, and we'll have a grand illumination.'

'All right, only nobody must look at anything till I come back.'

So I fetched my candles, and when Rosamund had lit them by tipping a lighted one against them (the grease then ran down on to the carpet, but we didn't mind) the room looked very gay. We huddled together on to the beds, and Rosamund commanded:

'Everybody to pull out together and only one thing at a time. Are you all ready? Now! One, two, three, go!'

I am afraid I have forgotten most of the things that came out of those stockings, except that Rosamund and I each got a clock. Hers was red and mine was blue, and they were called Bee clocks. They stood on little legs which we soon found could be unscrewed, and then the case came to pieces and the glass fell out and all the works could be seen. I also had a set of teeny little flower-pots about two inches high. There was a teeny watering can with them, and packets of mustard and cress seed. Later on when I was back in London, I followed the directions with the help of my governess, and the mustard and cress did actually grow and we ate it for tea.

But the thing that pleased me most was a glass swan exactly like Mrs Peabody's, except that while hers had red eyes, mine had green. I could hardly believe that it had come

to me already, without having to wait till I was grown up. I kissed it and put it beside my bed, next to my Bible, though not on top of it, as that would have been irreverent.

After breakfast I was told to go with the Savages to their mother's room where I should find the presents which my parents had sent for me. As we raced along the passage, a frantic quarrel broke out between Rosamund and Harry as to which of them was to be given an annual called *Little Folks*.

The Savages' mother had set out five chairs with heaps of presents on each, and we pounced down on them, Betty of course with a terrific squeal. I found that my presents were just what I wanted but what I thought I should never be given – beyond that I can't describe them.

Presents poured in at intervals throughout the day, but the only one I can remember was a life-size dachshund on wheels. Great-Uncle Algy gave it to Tommy, who at once broke into such howls of terror that it was quickly handed on to me who happened to be standing near. I had got past the age when people usually gave me stuffed animals, so I was very pleased to get this one. He was christened Great Agrippa and went to bed with me for years.

'Presents poured in at intervals throughout the day . . .' – one of the
chapter heading drawings from *Christmas with the Savages*

At one moment we all surged down into the dining room where the uncles and aunts were having their breakfast. One got to the dining room by going through a mysterious little room full of doors which was known as the lobby, and had a black and white marble floor and buffaloes' horns on the wall. One opened the biggest door and found oneself behind a screen, and when one had walked round the end of the screen, one found oneself in an immense room with pillars in it.

The grown-ups were eating at a big table in the middle, but there were wide open spaces all round them, and other tables near the walls. With a whoop, the Savages dashed towards a large polished table which stood in a corner and began playing ships on it and under it. I took in the situation at a glance and decided to follow an idea of my own and to go to the grown-up table where the people breakfasting would be at my mercy. I spotted an uncle whom I had not seen before and who I thought would find me irresistible, and I felt contempt for the Savages who were so childish that they chose to play ships under the sideboard at a time when they might have been fascinating the house-party.

Christmas at Tamerlane Hall, one of the drawings from
Mary Clive's book

Unfortunately for my plans, on my way towards my victim I had to pass near a table on which was a boar's head. The boar had rolling eyes and great tusks and I suppose was really only an ordinary pig, but it looked like something out of history. Round it was mashed jelly of a beautiful golden colour, and as no-one was looking at me I stuck two fingers in and took a great mouthful.

Then I was in a fix indeed. The jelly was perfectly horrible and I couldn't possibly bring myself to swallow it, but I didn't dare to spit it out. Instead of going to fascinate the grown-ups, I had to slink into the corner after the other children.

'Come up on deck, Evelyn,' said Rosamund, stretching out a hand.

But I ducked down into the cabin, where I found Harry and Peter.

'Which will you be,' said Harry, 'stoker or stewardess?' The Savages sometimes went to Ireland and so they knew about ships.

I nodded, still unable to open my mouth.

'What does that senseless sort of nod mean?' asked Harry. 'Does it mean you want to be a stoker and shovel coal till the perspiration pours off you in rivers, or does it mean that you want to be a stewardess and hand round basins?'

It really meant that I wished someone would hand *me* a basin, but at that moment the captain's head appeared upside down as he leant over from the deck, and while Harry and Peter were exchanging remarks with it, I managed to get rid of the jelly under the corner of the carpet which was fortunately not nailed down.

'I think I'll just be a passenger,' I said, 'a grand lady with lots of luggage and a pomeranian.'

'What class are you going?' asked Harry.

I said I should certainly go first-class. Peter now began

shovelling coal, and considering that the coal, the shovel and the furnace were all imaginary, he somehow managed to produce very loud and lifelike noises. I looked out of a porthole to see how the grown-ups were bearing it, but they were so wrapped up in themselves and their own breakfasts, that they did not seem to notice us at all.

'Land ahoy!' shouted Lionel's voice from the deck. 'Stop the ship! We're running on to a rock! Stop her, can't you, you donkeys.'

'Very sorry Captain,' shouted Rosamund. 'Afraid I can't! The wheel's stuck.'

'Stand by for a wreck!' shouted Lionel. 'Man the boats! Women and children first!' Here he threw Betty into the sea. She let out one of her most horrible yells and came rolling into the cabin.

'Rock's getting closer, getting closer,' shouted Lionel. 'Now I can see the houses, now I can see the people, now I can see the gulls, now I can see the winkles. And now for the beastly bump.'

As he spoke, the three children on the deck crashed together and there were shouts of 'Take to the boats!' 'Swim for your lives!' and also, less appropriately, 'Fire! Murder! Burglary!'

The whole lot of us (myself among them) were now swimming about on the carpet, but Lady Tamerlane had finished her breakfast.

'Run on, children, and get ready for church,' she said as she rose from the table, and as no-one ever thought of disobeying her, up we got and off we ran.

Getting ready for church took us a long time, particularly as the nurses could not agree as to whether we were to wear our Sunday clothes or not. I think in the end we wore our Sunday coats but not our Sunday hats, but somehow we were made to feel just as stiff and uncomfortable as if we were dressed entirely in Sunday outfits.

Ding, dong, dell, went the church bells.

'Hurry up Harry,' said Nana Savage languidly. 'There are the bells saying "Come to church! Come to church!"'

We stopped to listen, but at that moment the peal changed to Dinga-dinga-dong.

'But now they are saying "Go away from church! Go away from church!"' objected Harry.

We were shocked by Harry, and still more so by Betty who announced that she was going to take her golliwog to church. Indeed, this made us really anxious, as it was almost impossible to get Betty to change her mind once she had made it up, but to the relief of everybody she came to her senses in time. She said that after all she had decided that Golly was rather young for church, so instead she would leave him sitting on the dirty clothes basket so that he could have a nice cosy talk to it with no-one listening.

Eventually we got off and went in a straggling crowd down the avenue. The church stood by itself in the park, a little old church with cedar trees in the churchyard. The grass was neatly mown and the path was weeded and the graves were decorated with holly wreaths. Beside it was a big mound covered with trees which the children called the giant's castle. We never got the chance to explore it, so for all I know a giant really did live on top.

In church we filled several pews, the children being put in one against the back wall, which was a good thing as a great deal of whispering and giggling went on. I think children don't giggle as much now as they used to, perhaps because they are not so strictly brought up. When we were all in a pew, a ledge on a hinge was fixed across the opening so as to make more room, and the child who knelt in front of that, was always pushing his prayer book over it or else just catching it in time. In either case the rest of us giggled.

Peter and Betty shared a prayer book. They followed the

service closely, and whenever they came to a word they could read, they joined in as loudly as they could. Peter showed Betty what 'Amen' looked like, and they waited, panting, for every one, and then bawled it, generally coming in a second too soon or a second too late. Rosamund's prayer book was full of pretty little markers which kept slipping out and fluttering to the ground, followed by dives and head-bumping.

Harry behaved fairly well, although he occasionally asked questions in his usual voice without making any attempt to lower it, while Lionel behaved beautifully except during the carols. These he would sing to ridiculous words which he had picked up at school and which we all thought terribly witty.

I was in two minds whether to sit primly like the grown-ups or to wriggle and giggle like the children, and I tried first one way and then the other. Unfortunately Lady Tamerlane chose to look round just as I was laughing at Peggy waggling her finger through a hole in her glove, and she made me come out of the back pew and sit beside her for the rest of the service. I was covered with shame at this public disgrace, and thought that everyone in the church, from the clergyman to the old man who blew the organ, was looking at me with scorn.

However, I recovered my spirits on the way home, as one of the great-aunts walked beside me and talked to me as though nothing had happened. She told me stories of what she and her cousins had done when they were young, and I came to the conclusion that Victorian children, far from being little angels, were really much naughtier than we were. It was astonishing to learn that Great-Uncle Algy had mesmerized his governess and had then not been able to un-mesmerize her again, or that Lady Tamerlane herself had, when a little girl, gone into a visitor's bedroom and put soapy water in all her cupboards and drawers as a suggestion that she was staying too long. 'And once,' said the great-aunt in her little squeaky voice, 'we all decided to run away.'

I couldn't help laughing. We had dropped behind the others, as the great-aunt could hardly walk, and the idea of her running at all was absurd.

'Where were you going to run to?'

'We meant either to go to London to be crossing-sweepers, or to Malvern because the water was so good.'

'And what happened?'

'Gustavus always was a tell-tale-tit,' said the great-aunt, her dim eyes flashing as she looked at the bent back of an aged gentleman tottering along in front of us. I could see that she never had quite forgiven him for sneaking.

By the time I reached the house I had entirely got back my good opinion of myself and was able to eat as much turkey and Christmas pudding as anybody.

from

The Vision of Piers Ploughman

WILLIAM LANGLAND

Little factual evidence exists about the life of William Langland. He is thought to have been born in about 1332 in either Colwall or Ledbury, or possibly Cleobury Mortimer over

*the border in Shropshire, and lived until the end of the century.
A minor cleric of his day, and a contemporary of Chaucer, he
based his epic poetical work on a vision experienced while
resting on the slopes of the Herefordshire Beacon in the
'Malverne hulles'. It is primarily a story – often satirical – of
Christian justice, of the gulf between good and evil, and rich
and poor, which unfolds during the course of a series of vivid
'dreams'. Towards the end of the poem, Langland offers a
visionary account of the founding of the Christian Church,
which includes the following passage from the Nativity story. It
is told in the words of Conscience, who is attempting to explain
to the dreamer the meaning of this particular vision. The
original work, written in early English alliterative verse, is not
easy for the layman to understand, and this extract is from a
modern English prose translation.*

'But to speak more of the name *Christ*, and how he acquired
it. The truth is that His first name was simply *Jesus*. And
when he was born in Bethlehem, as the Scripture tells, and
came to take human nature, kings and angels worshipped
Him with the riches of the earth. First there came the angels
from heaven, who knelt and sang: "Gloria in excelsis Deo".
Then came the three kings, kneeling and offering Him myrrh
and abundance of gold. They did not ask for thanks, or for
anything in return, but came to acknowledge Him sovereign
of sun and earth and sea; and then they returned to their royal
kinsmen, guided on their way by angels.

'Thus the words which you quoted were fulfilled – "That at
the name of Jesus every knee should bow, of things in heaven, of
things on earth, and things under the earth". For all the angels
of heaven kneeled at His birth, and all the wisdom of the world
was in those three kings. And the gifts they offered were Reason,
Righteousness and Pity. Therefore the wise men of that time,
the Doctors and men of learning, called them the *Magi*.

The Herefordshire slopes of the Malvern Hills, where Langland
experienced the vision which led to his epic work

'The first king came with the gift of Reason, symbolized by incense. The second offered Righteousness, the counterpart of Reason, which seemed like red gold. For gold is like perpetual Loyalty, and Reason like rich gold, which stands for Righteousness and Truth. And the third king who came and knelt before Jesus offered Him Pity, signified by myrrh. For myrrh is a symbol of mercy and mildness of speech. So these three gifts, of equal worth, were offered together by the kings of three different peoples, all kneeling to Jesus.

'But despite all these precious gifts, our Lord and Prince Jesus was neither king nor conqueror until He began to grow to manhood and show His great wisdom. For a man who would be a Conqueror and leader of men must be a master of many skills and wiles, and possess great wisdom – as Jesus did in His life, if I had time to tell it.'

Bethlehem

ROBERT WADE

This amusing little Christmas poem is from a collection entitled Verses Written in Sussex and Herefordshire, *compiled and published in 1970 after the author had moved from the former county to the latter. It looks at a homely episode in the life of the infant Jesus in a decidedly new light.*

146

A Herefordshire Christmas

At bath time in Bethlehem Saint Joseph filled the tub
And blessed Mary fetched the soap her baby Lord to
  scrub,
And all the birds came singing round the windows and
  the door
And little lonely yellow frogs sat singing on the floor.

At bath time in Bethlehem the little fishes came
And swam into the bucket so that they might join the
  game,
And could you think of any toy to meet a baby's wish
So lovely for a bath time as a really truly fish?

At bath time in Bethlehem an angel made the bed
And warmed the pillows properly to rest a baby's head,
And when the Babe was carried in and tucked up warm
  and dry
The angel stayed and sat beside to sing a lullaby.

*From the same collection come these six seasonal lines which bear the
simple title 'For a Christmas Card'.*

The shining Kings, with pomp and praise,
Ride down through History to their fate;
This day that numbers all our days
Gives each his order and his date.

And still when we look back to them,
The Kings look back to Bethlehem.

Wassailing the Christmas Orchards

JOHN MASH

The custom of wassailing Herefordshire's apple orchards at Christmastime – once a sort of insurance policy to encourage an abundant crop at the next harvest – dates back many centuries. The old tradition still survives, perpetuated by the Leominster Morris Men who each year re-enact the age-old rituals among the orchards of today. Herefordshire writer John Mash recorded his impressions of just such an occasion in 1990.

They say only mad dogs and Englishmen go out in the midday sun, but long before Noel Coward, gatherings of 'pagan' Englishmen went out into the midwinter cold of Herefordshire's ancient apple orchards, with barrels of cider, shotguns and toast. It was a strange combination, but in fact it was all needed for wassailing the apple trees at Christmastime.

Long before the Victorians turned Christmas into a respectable family affair, our peasant forebears celebrated the midwinter solstice with feast days and riotous revels in the rural communities. Wassailing was one such feast, dating back to the Vikings, whose 'wassail' greeting was *Waes thu hal,* meaning 'To your health!'

In early times the wassail greeting was first called by the head of the household and then passed on to every member,

along with a large bowl, traditionally of maplewood, filled with hot mead spiced with sweet herbs. 'Lamb's Wool' was a particularly potent wassail brew, being a mixture of hot beer, wine, honey, spices, cream and roasted apples.

That is how it was for the wealthy. The poorer agricultural workers would take their wassail cup, decorated with evergreens, ribbons and tinsel, round to the richer houses in the village, first singing a carol, and then begging for alms and a drink.

Although, down the years, many of the old customs have largely died out, the wassailing of the apple trees is still being carried on in the ancient orchards of Herefordshire. In recent years, it has been saved through the efforts of the Leominster Morris Men who have wassailed the orchards of Symonds

The Leominster Morris Men kindle one of the ritual fires in a Herefordshire orchard, in their revival of the ancient Christmastide wassailing custom

Cider at Stoke Lacy, Dunkertons Cider at Pembridge, and Westons at Much Marcle.

It happens like this. A week after Christmas, the Morris Men foregather at the chosen location and lead a torchlight procession down dark country lanes to the orchards, where the assemblage waits in warm modern anoraks and wellies for the centuries-old ceremony to begin. Ben Bydawell of the Leominster Morris Men, top-hatted and decorated with sprigs of evergreen, explains what the cider, shotguns and toast are all about.

'We will dip the slices of toast in cider, and put them up among the branches of the apple trees,' he says. 'The shotguns are then fired up through the branches to ward off evil spirits. A libation of cider is poured over the roots of the trees, and also shared by all those gathered around, who will then circle the trees, dancing and singing, to bring fertility and good luck in the year to follow.'

> Here's health to our master and to his right eye.
> God send our master a good Christmas pie,
> A good Christmas pie that we may all see,
> To my wassailing bowl I drink unto thee!

Folklore has it that the cider-soaked toast was a gift, or sacrament, for the robins which were considered sacred birds in ancient mythology. The firing of the volley of shots would awaken the god of the apple trees from his midwinter sleep. Earlier wassailers would blow cows' horns, beat the trees with sticks, and bang bowls or kettles – anything to make a din and frighten the evil spirits.

Wassailing the apple trees was originally a family occasion. The cider-soaked toast was presented by the oldest member, but all the family had to be present, or bad luck would surely follow. Certainly it was a serious affair, emphasising the family's dependence on the apple harvest.

Today, only the ceremony remains, but time has perhaps enriched the magic and renewed the ancient pagan spirit which flickers in the shadowy orchards as the Morris Men prepare for the next part of the custom, the lighting of the first of thirteen fires.

'The thirteen fires around the apple trees represent Christ and the twelve apostles,' Ben Bydawell explains. 'The so-called Judas fire is immediately extinguished, leaving twelve, one for each month of the year – and at the centre of the burning circle, we rekindle the sun by lighting a dry bush.'

And so with the toast offered, the volley of shots sounded, and the fires lit, you can almost feel the touch of centuries past, with Herefordshire hiding in the darkness beyond the circle of firelight.

Afterwards, as we disperse into the night through the dark orchards, we make our way to the local hostelry where the

'And now good folk our play is done . . .' The Leominster Morris Men end a performance of a traditional Christmas Mummers' play

traditional evening will continue with the Leominster Morris Men performing the ancient Mummers' play, which was traditionally acted by out-of-work farm labourers in the winter to raise money.

The tree-spirit magic of the orchards is forgotten now, as past and present meet. The Morris Men hurriedly produce costumes from the boots of cars, and the characters in the Mummers' play emerge. They include a black-faced Father Christmas, Napolean, Robin Hood and St George – a cast of heroes which has evolved over the years and which is changing still. Ribald reference to the heroes and villains of today are also added. Who cares? In the play they end up, as tradition demands, killed and brought back to life – reborn, just as the sun is at the midwinter solstice.

Acknowledgements

Introductory sections are by David Green, using published and unpublished reference material and personal interviews.

The poem 'The Weobley Goose' is from *Poems of the Wye and Herefordshire District* published by Cornish Bros Ltd in 1937. The extract from *A Funny Old Quist* is reproduced by courtesy of Clive Murphy and Mary Hancox; the book, originally published by Dobson Books, was issued as a paperback in 1986 by Eland. 'A Christmas Tonic' by Sid Wright is reproduced by permission of *The Grocer*. The extracts from *The Burton Court Recipes* (published by Logaston Press) are reproduced by permission of Helen J. Simpson. *Christmas Customs* by A. Lowndes Moir is quoted by courtesy of the author's family. The entries from *The Diary of a Farmer's Wife, 1796–1797* (Penguin, 1981) are reproduced by permission of Penguin Books Ltd (© Mollie Preston, 1937, 1964, 1980). The poems of John Masefield and the extract from his book *The Box of Delights* are reproduced by courtesy of the Society of Authors as the literary representative of the estate of John Masefield. The Woolhope Club is acknowledged for the extract from the Reverend James Davies's paper 'Old Herefordshire Customs'. The poem by Lady Elgar is included by courtesy of the Elgar Birthplace Trust. The extract from *Daughter of Wyedean and Kernow* by Jessie M. Stonham is reprinted with the permission of the author. Mary Hannah Herman's *Lady Jenny*, published by Square One Publications, is quoted by permission of the author. The carols 'The Holy Well' and 'On Christmas Day' are from *Twelve Traditional Carols from Herefordshire* published by Stainer & Bell. The chapter from *Tales of Old Ross* is reproduced by courtesy of *The Ross Gazette*. The passage from *Boy at The Commercial* by Alick Rowe is included with the permission of Faber & Faber who published the book in 1978. The story of the 'Holy Thorns' of Wye by Hal Bethell first appeared in *Herefordshire The County Magazine* and is reprinted by permission of the author. H.P. Bulmer Drinks Ltd of Hereford are acknowledged for the three recipes from *Cider For All Seasons*. The assistance of Jill Jones with historical research for Howard Browne's Hereford Boy Bishop story is gratefully acknowledged. *Christmas With the Savages* by Mary Clive was first published by Macmillan and the extract is reproduced by

courtesy of the author. The passage from *The Vision of Piers Ploughman* is from the translation by J.F. Goodridge published by Penguin Books Ltd in 1959 and revised in 1966 (© J.F. Goodridge 1959 and 1966). 'Wassailing the Christmas Orchards' by John Mash, first appeared in *Worcestershire & Herefordshire The County Magazine* and is reproduced with the author's permission.

Although considerable effort has been made to trace and contact original authors, this has not proved possible in every case. To those writers who have remained elusive, the compiler and publishers offer grateful acknowledgement for the extracts reproduced.

Picture Credits

Opposite page 1 – By courtesy of the Kilvert Society. Page 15 – Scraperboard drawing by Peter Manders, reproduced by courtesy of Helen J. Simpson. Pages 18, 95 – *Hereford Times*. Pages 23, 127 – By courtesy of Jill Jones. Pages 31, 76, 145 – Bill Meadows. Page 33 – Birmingham Reference Library. Pages 37, 131 – Marjorie Wight Collection at Herefordshire County Records Office. Pages 41, 92 – By John Tilley, reproduced by courtesy of David Postle. Page 51 – The National Trust. Page 56 – Elgar Birthplace Trust. Page 84 – By Eric Crooks, reproduced by courtesy of 6000 Locomotive Association. Page 90 – *Ledbury Reporter*. Pages 99, 109, 114, 119, 129 – Hereford Library. Page 105 – *Herefordshire The County Magazine*. Pages 122, 123 – H.P. Bulmer Drinks Ltd. Pages 134, 137, 138 – By courtesy of Lady Mary Clive. Pages 149, 151 – Leominster Morris Men/John Mash.